The Sailing Ships of New England

1607-1907

By
JOHN ROBINSON
Curator of the Marine Room, Peabody Museum of Salem

and

GEORGE FRANCIS DOW
Curator of the Society for the Preservation of New England Antiquities

Skyhorse Publishing

www.skyhorsepublishing.com

10 9 8 7 6 5 4 3 2 1

Library of Congress Cataloging-in-Publication Data

Robinson, John, 1846-1925.
  The sailing ships of New England, 1607-1907 / by John Robinson and George Francis Dow.
       p. cm.
  Originally published: Salem, Mass. : Marine Research Society, 1922. (Publication ; no. 1).
  ISBN-13: 978-1-60239-039-3 (pbk. : alk. paper)
  ISBN-10: 1-60239-039-8 (pbk. : alk. paper)
  1. Sailing ships--New England. 2. Shipping--New England. I. Dow, George Francis, 1868-1936. II. Title.

VM23.R6 2007
623.8220974'0903--dc22

Printed in Canada

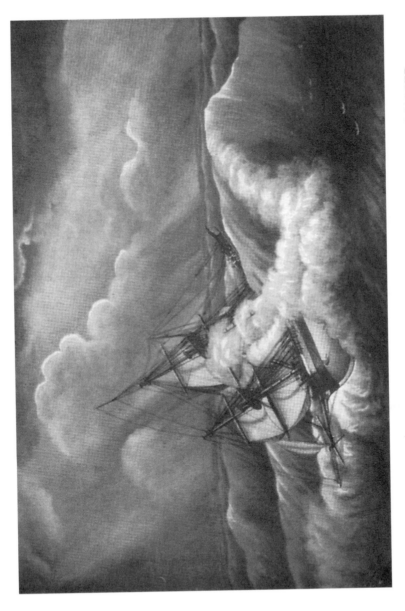

SNOW "AMERICA" OF MARBLEHEAD, ARCHIBALD SELMAN, MASTER.
ON MONDAY, JANUARY 2, 1803.

AFTER A WATER-COLOR BY M. CORNE

DEDICATED TO
CAPT. ARTHUR H. CLARK
WHO SET SAIL FOR HIS LAST PORT
BEFORE HE COULD COMPLETE HIS
WORK INTENDED FOR
THIS VOLUME

PREFACE

UNTIL recent times the sailing ship has been so vital a factor in the life and development of New England that every fireside has felt in some degree the influence of its commercial intercourse with nearly every port in the known world. It is natural, therefore, that the descendants of the sailors and merchants of earlier days should inherit an interest in the ways of the old-time ship and seek to know more about the building, rigging and sailing of the various types of vessels that once brought adventure and a livelihood to many a New England boy. That interest has led to the preservation in a number of the old sea ports, of museum collections devoted to the commercial marine. Numerous private collections of ship pictures, ship models, marine objects and books relating to the ship and to the sea are also being made not only in all parts of New England but throughout the United States.

The Marine Research Society has been organized at Salem, Massachusetts, for the purpose of collecting and publishing worthwhile material relating to the ship, its construction, rig and navigation; to the ways of the sailor and his adventures in uncharted seas; to the days of the pirates and the merchant adventurers; and to any other matter of general interest that pertains to the commercial marine. In this connection it is also proposed to reprint certain publications that have now become rare and are inaccessible to the average collector in this field. It is the aim of the Society to restrict its work to the publication of matter of scientific or historical value and it thereby hopes to deserve and receive the co-operation of serious students of maritime subjects so that the results of their investigations may become known through its Publications.

This volume, the initial Publication of the Society, should find a wide appeal because of the lively, present-day interest in the old-time ship picture, and it has only been made possible through the generous co-operation of museums and private collectors of these interesting and oft-times curious pictorial representations of the sailing vessels of other days. While many of the ship pictures in the volume are here reproduced for the first time, a considerable number have been in-

5

cluded through the kind permission of authors and publishers. This accounts for the great variation in size of the engraved blocks. It should also be borne in mind that many original ship pictures have become stained and discolored so that it is now impossible to obtain good results when they are reproduced. It has been the aim to include in this volume pictures of vessels built, owned or commanded by New England men.

Numerous friends have aided in the preparation of this volume and the Society is under particular obligation to Mr. Charles H. Taylor, Jr., of Boston, for making available the resources of his collection of ship pictures,—probably the largest collection in private hands in New England and containing numerous examples of the work of the artists about the Mediterranean. He has also generously supplied the colored frontispiece reproducing for the first time an early water-color in his collection. The Peabody Museum and the Essex Institute, at Salem, have loaned engraved blocks used in their publications and co-operated in other ways. The ship pictures that have appeared from time to time in the valuable historical series published by the State Street Trust Company of Boston, are here included by the kind permission of Mr. Allan Forbes and Mr. Perry Walton. Cordial thanks are also due to Mr. Hollis French, Horace Gray, M. D., Mr. Arthur F. Harlow, Mr. William R. Hedge, Mr. James A. Hutchinson, Joseph Morrill, Esq., Messrs. Houghton Mifflin Company, Messrs. Little, Brown & Co., the Bostonian Society, the Massachusetts Historical Society, and the Society for the Preservation of New England Antiquities, all of Boston; Dr. Alfred Johnson, Mrs. Herbert Foster Otis, and Prof. Charles S. Sargent, all of Brookline; Mr. Francis W. Sprague of Cambridge; Oliver H. Howe, M. D. of Cohasset; and to all others who have in any way furthered the production of this volume.

TABLE OF CONTENTS

THE SAILING SHIPS OF NEW ENGLAND

1607—1907

NEW England, with its many rivers and long indented coast-line, has always been a breeding place for sailors and a natural location for shipbuilding. The early settlers along the shore-line found no extent of rich soil awaiting cultivation and of necessity turned to fishing and to trade. The forests close at hand supplied the best of timber for building vessels and on the sea a fishing industry and a trade with England and the West Indies soon brought prosperity to the colonies.

Probably the first vessel to be built in New England was the *Virginia,* a "faire pinnace of thirty tons," launched in the spring of 1607 at the

FIRST VESSEL
BUILT IN
NEW ENGLAND

mouth of the Kennebec river in Maine. It was built by the newly founded Popham Colony and after some voyaging along shore and sailing up the Kennebec as far as the head of navigation, to what is now Augusta, it set sail for England when the settlement was abandoned in the fall of that year and arrived safely. This small vessel afterwards made several voyages across the Atlantic and in June, 1610, was lying at anchor at Point Comfort, Virginia, when Lord De La Warre arrived, it having brought over a part of the Gates and Somers expedition in August of the previous year.

In the museum of the Pilgrim Society at Plymouth, Massachusetts, is preserved the hull of the small sloop *Sparrow Hawk,* which sailed from London for Virginia, with passengers, in the fall of 1626 and was wrecked near Plymouth. The sands of Cape Cod safely preserved, until recent years, the keel and ribs of this, the earliest known sailing vessel that has survived in New England. She was only forty feet long and the emigrants who crossed the Atlantic in her, most of them un-familiar with the sea and its moods, certainly were not lacking in personal courage or faith in their destiny.

The *Sparrow Hawk* was forty feet in length, and had a breadth of beam of twelve feet and ten inches, and a depth of nine feet and seven and one-half inches. Her keel measured twenty-eight feet and ten inches and the rake of her stern-post was four inches to the foot. "Her forward lines are convex, her after lines sharp and concave, and her midship section is almost the arc of a circle."* She had a square stern and a single mast located about midship for there is a hole in the keelson showing where it was stepped. The rig probably was a lateen yard with a triangular sail. Her planking was English oak, two inches thick and most of it ten inches wide.

An early need at the Plymouth Colony was a ship-carpenter and one was sent over in the spring of 1624. Governor Bradford records

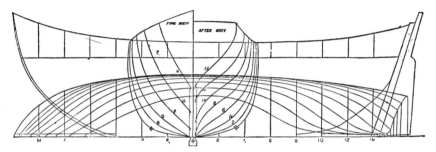

DRAFT OF THE LINES OF THE HULL OF THE "SPARROW-HAWK,"
MADE IN 1865 BY D. J. LAWLER.

that "he quickly builte them 2 very good & strong shalops (which after did them greate service), and a greate and strong lighter, and had hewne timber for 2 catches ; but that was lost, for he fell into a feaver in ye hote season of that yeare [1624] . . . and dyed." It was one of these shallops that was sent to the Kennebec river in the fall of the next year to open up a trade in furs with the Indians, a trade that eventually relieved the Pilgrims from their financial difficulties and extricated them from the clutches of the Merchant Adventurers in London. The Governor writes that "bigger vessel had they none. They had laid a little deck over her midships to keepe ye corne drie, but ye men were faine to stand it out all weathers without shelter ; and yt time of ye year begins to growe tempestious." Their ship-carpenter was dead but a house-carpenter sawed their larger shallop in halves, lengthened and decked her over and rebuilt her into a small

*Report of Messrs. Dolliver & Sleeper, ship-builders, of Boston, made in 1865 at the time the wreck was uncovered. See "Loss of the Sparrow-Hawk in 1626," Boston, 1865.

pinnace that did good service for seven years. Later, the Colony bought an English trading ship, the "White Angel," and a fishing vessel that had been fitted out in England to fish under the English custom of shares.

The Company of the Massachusetts Bay early recognized the need for shipbuilding in the new colony and in their first general letter of instructions to John Endecott, dated April 17, 1629, wrote:

"We haue sent six Shipwrights, of whom Robert Molton is cheif . . . desiring that their labour may bee employed 2/3 for the generall Companie, and 1/3 for Mr. Cradock and his Assotiats." On May 28th following, the Company wrote directing that "The provisions for building of Shipps, as Pitch, Tar, Rozen, Okum, old ropes for Okum, Cordage, & Saylcloth, in all these Shipps, with 9 fferkins and 5 halfe barrells of Nayles in the *4 Sisters,* are 2/3 for the Companie in generall, and 1/3 for the Gouernor, Mr. Cradock, and his partners; as is also charge of one George Farr, now sent over to the six Shipwrights formerly sent. Our desire is a Storehouse may be made apart for the provisions of the Shipwrights and their Tooles, whereof Robert Moulton to haue the cheife Charge, and an Inventory to bee sent vs of all the Tooles, the new by themselues and the old by themselues, that was sent ouer for the vse of the said Shipwrights, or any of them, in these and the former shipps; . . . and our desire is, that these men bee kept at worke togeather, adding to their helpe such of the Companye's servants as you shall fynde needfull, & proportionably 1/2 as many of Mr. Cradock's, which course wee hold most equall; and that accordingly as any vessells bee built, first that both partyes may bee accomodated for the present occasion; but soe soone as 3 Shallops shalbe finished, two of them to bee sett out for the Companie, by lott, or as you shall agree there to make an equall devision, and one for our Gournor & his partners."

At the outset, the great need for housing the immigrants seems to have occupied the energies of Robert Moulton and his company of ship-carpenters and so far as known nothing was done about building the three shallops ordered by the Company. Shipbuilding in Massachusetts really began with the launching at Medford, on July 4, 1631, of Governor Winthrop's trading vessel, *The Blessing of the Bay,* which was built mainly of locust. He records that the "bark being of thirty tons went to sea," Aug. 31, 1631 and the following October she "went on a voyage to the eastward," and soon engaged in trade with the Dutch at New Amsterdam. An eighteen-ton pinnace brought Virginia corn and tobacco to Salem in 1631 and the same

"THE BLESSING OF THE BAY"

year a ship was built at Richmond Island, off Cape Elizabeth, Maine, which made regular voyages for some years between that trading settlement and England. This probably was the first regular packet service in the Colonies. In 1634, a pinnace of fifty tons came to Boston from Maryland loaded with corn to exchange for fish. In July, 1634, Capt. John Mason wrote to the Secretary of the Admiralty that more than fifty ships were trading to New England, of which "six sail of ships at least, if not more, belong to them."

Governor Winthrop when writing in his "Journal" of *The Blessing of the Bay,* always mentions her as a bark. As the bark-rigged vessel of to-day was unknown at the time, the question naturally arises, "What was the rig of the *Blessing?*" The Governor generally did not use the word in its purely literary sense as throughout his "Journal" he seemingly differentiates in mentioning the rigs of different vessels. His "barks" ranged from twelve to forty tons in size and were both "small" and "large." In 1636, a "bark" of twenty tons met John Oldham's "small pinnace," near Block Island and four years later a pinnace called the "Coach," on her voyage from Salem to New Haven, sprang a leak near Cape Cod, when "one Jackson, a godly man and an experienced seaman, laying the bark upon the contrary side, they fell to getting out the water" and safely returned to Salem. A "small Norsey bark of twenty-five tons," arrived in Boston in 1635 bound for the mouth of the Connecticut river. She had had a very stormy voyage but brought safely fourteen passengers, including two women, with their goods. They arrived four days too late, for Winthrop had already sent a "bark" with carpenters and workmen to take posession before the Dutch came.

In 1689, Capt. Cyprian Southack of Boston, captured in the Channel near the French coast and brought to Boston, a "small Ship or Barque called the St. John Frigott," of 40 tons. She belonged to Quebec and was condemned as a prize.

On the other hand, Edward Johnson of Woburn, writing in 1650, relates that "many a fair ship had her framing and finishing here, besides lesser vessels, barques and ketches; many a Master, besides common Seamen, had their first learning in this Colony."

In the Essex County Quarterly Court Records are filed the papers in a suit brought in 1666 in connection with the building of a "barke," containing items showing costs of "a fore mast and maine yard," and labor in "seeling the cabin."

In a list of twenty-seven vessels that arrived or cleared at Boston between Aug. 16, 1661 and Feb. 25, 1662 and had given bonds for customs, were ships of 60 to 150 tons burden, "barcques," of 30 to 50 tons, ketches of 16 to 30 tons, a "pincke" of 30 tons, and vessels of unnamed rig in tonnage from 40 to 150 tons.—*Massachusetts Archives,* Vol. 60, leaf 34.

By the year 1641 shipbuilding had become of such importance in the Colony that the Great and General Court adopted the following order :—

"Whereas the country is nowe in hand with the building of ships, which is a busines of great importance for the common good, & therefore sutable care is to bee taken that it bee well performed, according to the commendable course of England, & other places, it is therefore ordered that, when any ship is to bee built within this iurisdiction, it shalbee lawfull for the owners to appoint & put in some able man to survey the worke & workmen from time to time, as is usual in England ; & the same shall have liberty & power as belongs to his office, & if the ship-carpenter shall not, upon his advice, reforme & amende any thing which hee shall find to bee amise, then, upon complaint to the Governor, or Deputy, or any other 2 magistrates, they shall appoint 2 of the most sufficient ship carpenters of this iurisdiction, & shall give them authority from time to time (as neede shall require) to take veiw of every such ship, & all worke thereto belonging, & to see it bee performed & carried on according to the rules of their arte ; & for this end an oath shalbee administered to them, to bee faithfull & indifferent between the owners & workmen ; & their charges to bee borne by such as shalbee found in default ; & these veiwers shall have power to cause any bad timbers, or other insufficient worke or materialls, to bee taken out & amended, & all that they shall iudge to bee amisse to bee reformed at the charge of them through whose fault it growes."

In 1639, the same Court exempted ship-carpenters, fishermen (during the fishing season) and millers from compulsory military training.

The shallop is frequently mentioned in the early records. It was a small vessel having a mainmast, foremast and lug sails and used in fishing and coasting. They were good sailers.*

THE
SHALLOP

In 1630, when the ship bearing Winthrop and his company of settlers neared Cape Ann, they "met a shallop, which stood from Cape Ann towards the Isles of Shoals, which belonged to some English fishermen," and the

*The French shallop is a large sloop its mast carrying a gaff-mainsail. A small mast is often fixed abaft that carries a mizzen.

next morning they were boarded by Mr. Allerton from a shallop bound to Pemaquid and an hour later another shallop came out to meet them as they stood in by Baker's Isle to the harbor at Naumkeag, now Salem. In the spring of 1640, one Palmer, of Hingham, "an ancient and skilful seaman," in his ten-ton shallop, was overset in Boston harbor. Some one on board "had the sheet in his hand and let fly," but there being little ballast in her the shallop turned over and the men aboard climbed upon her side and soon after were taken off by a passing pinnace. In 1635, "a great shallop," carrying goods, was wrecked on Cape Ann during a northeasterly snow storm and about the same time a shallop bound for Salem laden with goods worth £100, was lost off Plymouth harbor. In 1648, "a shallop having been fishing at Monhigen and returning with other boats," the wind failing missed her way and split upon a rock. "The other boats fell to their oars and so escaped a like fate."

When Rev. Francis Higginson set sail for New England in the spring of 1629 he records in his journal of the voyage that after his ship, the *Talbot,* of three hundred tons, left the Needles, "wee tooke in our long boate & Shalope." A month later, when approaching the coast, "ye master of our shipp hoisted out ye shalop" to investigate "a great deale of froth" seen in the distance fearing "it might bee some breach of water."

Not infrequently the shallop was decked over, in whole or in part. In 1670 an agreement was made between Erasomus James, carpenter, of Marblehead, and the owners of a "boat or shallop" by which he was to rebuild the same "god sending him life & conuiant weather to worke in." The shallop was to be rebuilt one whole strake higher than her first build; he was to put in new planks where needed, to seal it, make up the rooms and do all other axe work within board and fit for sea excepting anchor stocks, oars, masts, yards, tiller and chimney.

On April 8, 1675, the Governor and Council of the Massachusetts Bay appointed a committee of three men to appraise two shallops, prizes brought in by Captain Mosely. The shallop *Edward & Thomas,* with its "masts & yards & a boate," was valued at £40. and mention is made of standing and running rigging, a mainsail of about ninety yards, a foresail of about forty-five yards, two cables, two anchors, an iron pot and pot hooks, a compass and a pump. The shallop *Penobscot,* "that Roads went out in," must have been a small vessel and perhaps in poor condition for "The Hull Masts & Canoe" were valued at only £6. A mainsail, old foresail and a bonnet, are listed. —*Massachusetts Archives,* Vol. 61, leaf 83.

"A French built shallop with a Topsail," owned in Salem and fishing off Block Island in the spring of 1704 was mistaken for a French privateer and an armed expedition was sent out from Newport, R. I., to effect her capture.

In a 1724 log-book of the "good sloop Sarah," on a voyage from the Island of Jersey to Cape Ann, mention is made of sighting off Cape Sable, "two Shallops & one Skooner of Marblehead."

The pinnace was another type of small vessel in common use in the early Colonial days not only for fishing and coasting but also for longer voyages to Bermuda and the West Indies. It was sharp at both ends, usually had two masts, and was the ancestor of the pinky and Chebacco boat so commonly used by New England fishermen during the 18th and early 19th centuries. Pinnaces varied in size from a few tons to vessels similar to the "Dove," a pinnace of fifty-two tons that arrived in Boston in 1634 from Maryland. The same year "an open pinnace," belonging to Ipswich, was cast away at the head of Cape Ann and another "open pinnace," returning from a voyage to Connecticut, was wrecked near Plymouth. This proves that this type of vessel sometimes was without a deck or at least was half-decked. Pinnaces frequently made the long voyage to London and sometimes made it more quickly than ships sailing at the same time. In 1636, a thirty-ton pinnace arrived in Boston from London three weeks before its accompanying ship. Both experienced very rough weather during the voyage. The next year "a small pinnace of thirty tons, which had been forth eight months, and was given up for lost," arrived in Boston harbor. She had sailed for Bermuda but storms had driven her down to Hispaniola and not daring to go into any inhabited place the men had gone ashore in obscure places and lived on turtles and hogs. She brought back tallow, hides, etc. and also an "aligarto" which was given to Governor Winthrop. In the summer of 1636, John Oldham, who came to Plymouth in 1623, was killed by Indians while on a trading voyage to Block Island in a small pinnace which had hatches, was built of boards an inch thick, and had a "little room underneath the deck."

THE PINNACE

In August, 1636, two pinnaces (one of them of forty tons burthen and built of cedar at Barbadoes) arrived at Boston from Virginia, loaded with fourteen heifers and about eighty goats having lost over twenty goats on the voyage.

The sloop was another rig in common use in the early days and with the growth of commercial intercourse with the West Indies it shared the carrying trade with numerous ketches and a sprinkling of brigantines and barks which in size were seldom in excess of fifty tons. The ketches usually were built with round sterns, the others with square sterns like the ships of the period. The sloops were built with a cabin on deck at the stern suggesting in appear-

THE SLOOP   ance the high poop decks to be seen in shipping of an earlier date and this resemblance was heightened by the long bowsprit pitched high in the air. The single mast of the sloop carried not only a fore-and-aft mainsail boom but one and sometimes two yards for topsails. Preserved in the *Massachusetts Archives* is a register of "ships and vessels" built in the Province between the years 1681 and 1714, totalling 1,332 vessels. Of this number over one hundred were built at Newbury at the mouth of the Merrimac river. Among these were sixteen ships, most of them built for London owners, and a "ship or barque" of fifty tons burthen. There were six barques, nine ketches, thirty brigantines, sixty-nine sloops and the "Snow or Barke Sea Flower, Boston, Pinke sterned, about 20 Tons, built in 1709."

In 1707, William Clifton, a merchant of Surinam, instructed his agent at Salem, Mass., to have built on his account a sloop of forty-five foot keel, eighteen and a half feet wide and nine feet deep, to be built Rhode Island fashion with a round house and to be named the "Johanna or Seaflower." When completed she was to sail for Surinam with the following cargo: "Sixteen large horses of 4 or 5 year old and not aboue it with long Tailes; fifty thousand red Oake Staues, three thousand foot boards fitt for heading, five & Twenty barrells with onyons, five & Twenty pound Shalotes, five thousand pound Virginia Bright leafe tobacco, Twelue ferkins of new Butter, Six barrells of beafe, Six Sett of Truss hoops & 300 Truss hoop nails, one frame of a boat of 25 foot keel, 10 foot wide & 3 1/2 foot deep, without any planke . . . You must hyre your men for Surinam & from thence to Madera or Ireland."

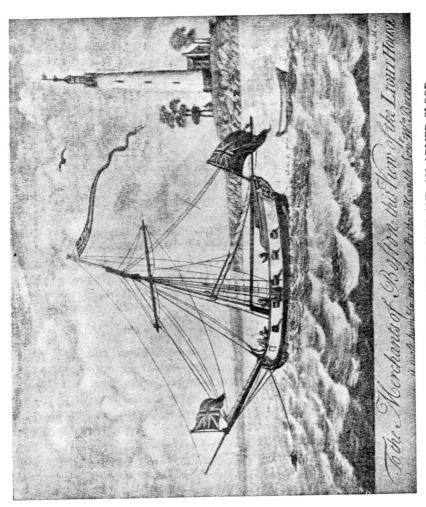

VIEW OF THE BOSTON LIGHTHOUSE AND AN ARMED SLOOP.

From the mezzotint after a drawing by William Burgis of Boston, made in 1729 and now in the possession of the United States Light House Board.   The only known example.

In 1697, the sloop *Hope,* of Salem, 30 tons burthen, was hired under an agreement that "said Sloop should be fitted with Good Masts* Boome Sails Anchors Cables & all Apurtenances Suitable for such a vessel for a voyage to Pensilvaniah, Virginia & Maryland & so to Salem again for four months."

In the eighteenth century Boston newspapers frequent references to sloops may be found among the news items. In the Feb. 26 - Mar. 5, 1704/5 issue of the *Boston News-Letter* appears the advertisement of a good sloop for fishing for sale at £25. The sloop "will carry six Cord of Wood without taking down her rooms" and was well furnished with rigging, etc. including a canoe.

In the fall of 1729 there was found at sea off Cape Cod, a sloop, bottom up, "Rhode Island built, with a blue Stern, two Cabbin Windows, her Counter painted yellow with two black ovals, and he thinks her sides were painted yellow, her Keel was about 40 foot, and her bottom Tallow'd. Her Counter had been Cork'd & Pey'd with Pitch over the Paint & not scrap'd off. Her Mouldings were all white. She had lost her mast, bowsprit and rudder." Two years later the sloop *Maryland,* of Boston, bound for Philadelphia, was struck by lightning and lost at sea. "The candle went out in the Binnicle . . . the Coat of the Mast about the Partners† was torn to Pieces and the Water was up to a man's Middle in the Steerage." In 1747, a Newport, R. I. vessel reported a wreck off Nantucket, a sloop of about sixty tons with a white bottom, blue stern and hants,‡ four cabbin windows with white moulding around them, two timber heads on the stern, a plank sheer as far as the quarter deck. Hanging to the main sheet was "a sounding Line in a Conger, and in it a Lock of Carolina Moss." Undoubtedly the sloop drifted into the Gulf Stream and was swept north.

In the July 5, 1753 issue of the *Boston News-Letter* is printed a description of the sloop *Nancy,* William Shearer, master, seized by the crew in the river Gambia, with a piratical design. The sloop probably was a slaver. The description is as follows: "Built in the

*Probably meaning mainmast and topmast.

†The coat was a piece of tarred canvas nailed around the mast at the deck to prevent water from running down between decks. The partners were pieces of plank fastened in a framework at the opening in the deck through which the mast passed and were intended to strengthen the deck at that point and relieve pressure from the mast.

‡Hances: falls or descents of the fife-rails from the stern to the gangways.

Colony of Connecticut, Burthen 70 Tons, nine Months old, deep waisted, six Ports of a side, five of which are open, and painted with Vermillion, mounted with four Guns, one Pounders, two Quarter Scuttles Vermillion painted from the upper part of the Port to the lower part; the outside is painted black, and freez'd with Pearl colour, very large Freeze; the upper Streak on the Round house plain Vermillion; the Streak below that green, with a small yellow Freeze; Square-Stern, painted the same; under her Counter blue, with yellow Curtains; and steers with a Wheel; has no Register or Custom-House Papers or any other Papers relating to the Cargo."

In 1744, a "Bumpkin* sloop" was advertised for sale in the *Boston News-Letter.* In 1772, the sloop *George,* owned by Aaron Lopez of Neport, R. I., was lying at Jamaica, W. I., unfit for a voyage "owing to the Badness of her Sails . . . the Dementions of the Main Sail is as follows the Hight of the Mast 44 feet and Length of the Boom 49 Do. the hight of the Jibb 62 feet and the Bowl Split 25 feet."†

A wrecked sloop sighted off New York harbor in 1761 had "a winlace quite new, and steered in her cabin."

Incidental allusion has already been made to the canoe. It is frequently mentioned in connection with shipping in the early days and curiously enough we now have little exact information as to its size or lines. The white birch from which the Indian canoe is made grows but sparsely as far south as Massachusetts.

THE CANOE   Generally the name is applied to a dugout made from a log—the crudest form of a boat known to all races. This probably was the type of boat that overset in the North river at Salem, on July 2, 1630, and caused the death of Henry Winthrop, the son of the Governor.‡ In the Governor's *Journal* may be found frequent mention of canoes, seemingly small tenders to vessels, sometimes small boats in and about the harbor and sometimes boats used for fishing or gunning. In 1707, a fishing sloop at Wells,

---

*The bumkin was a short boom or beam of timber projecting from the bow by which to extend the lower edge of the foresail to the windward.

†Commerce of Rhode Island, Vol. I, p. 401.

‡At Salem "they crosse these rivers with small Cannowes, which are made of whole pine trees, being about two foot & a half over, and 20 foote long; in these likewise they goe a fowling, sometimes two leagues to sea; there be more Cannowes in this towne than in all the whole Patent; every household having a water-house or two." Woods' *New Englands Prospect,* London, 1634.

Maine, containing three men, filled in the heavy sea and the men were drowned as "no canoe could approach them by reason of the Rage of the Sea." Seven years later, one Cockrum, "with 20 men fitted out in a Cannoe from Providence" (in the Bahamas) was committing piracies on the Florida coast.

In September 1730, a reward of £4 was offered in the *Boston News-Letter* for the recovery of "a Mohogany Canoe, taken away from the North End, 21 Foot long, square stern, sharp head, places to row with 5 Oars, flat bottom, stern sheets and fore sheets, two places for masts, several timbers in her Red Wood, made out of a whole Tree, one pintle* and another Iron, her main Tho't knee'd." Here is something specific. Yet, the comma after the word *Wood,* if correctly inserted, would seem to indicate that this large and well-equipped sailing boat was dug out of a single tree.

Sloops and other small vessels frequently were equipped with a canoe which served as a tender and it is not unusual to find a full-rigged ship supplied with a canoe. In February, 1734, Captain Waterhouse sailed from Portsmouth N. H., and was overtaken by a storm. A heavy sea "so far overset the ship, that the top of the lee Pump was in the Water." The mizzen mast was cut away and she righted, but three men were killed and "a canoe that was lashed to Windward coming across him broke the Master's thigh."

In 1761, Remember Preston of Dorchester, while returning home from Castle William, in Boston harbor, was drowned by the oversetting of his canoe. When found the next morning the sail was still standing in the canoe; the oars and benches were found on Spectacle island.

Following the shallop, pinnace and sloop, eighteenth-century New England built a great variety of one and two-masted boats variously named and generally used in the fisheries. In the Oct. 4/11, 1733 issue of the *Boston News-Letter* is advertised for sale "a Large Two Mast Boat, well fitted and deck'd, with two Suits of Two-Masted Sails, a good Road and Anchor, with an Iron Hearth." Boats In May, 1757, Arthur Savage advertised to sell at public vendue on the north side of the Town Dock, Boston, "Two Pinck-Stern'd two Mast Boats—one ditto square-sterned, with Masts, Rigging and Sails, and one Moses, all lying in the Town-

*A metal bolt fastened on the back of the rudder by which to hang it to the stern post.

Dock above the Bridge. One other Pinck-stern'd two Mast Boat, with rigging and sails, lying at Mr. Thomas Bentley's, Boat-builder, at the North End."

The pink, so named for its sharp stern, varied in size. In 1691, "the Pink, or Buss,* Two Brothers," with its cargo of salt, raisins, brimstone, oil and wine, brought into Boston from Europe, was seized by the Collector, for violation of the Acts of Trade, but a sympathetic jury brought in a verdict of "not guilty." "A new pink vessel," of 46 foot keel, 9 1/2 foot hold, 18 foot breadth, 3 feet 9 inches between decks, burthen 80 tons, built at Portsmouth, N. H., was advertised for sale in the June 11 - 18, 1711 issue of the *Boston News-Letter.*

THE PINK

Winthrop records in his *Journal,* the arrival in Boston, in May, 1633, of a Dutch pink that had been trading to the southward. In 1648, a Dutch "hoy", a two-masted vessel, of about thirty tons, reached Boston with seven men in her and a cargo of cordage and other goods. She made the voyage from the Isle of Wight in five weeks. John Hull, the mint-master, owned parts in several pinks trading with the West Indies and Europe, and Jonathan Corwen, the Salem merchant, owned the pink *John and Elizabeth,* which made a voyage to Bilboa in 1678 loaded with dried fish for the Roman Catholic population of that city. The pink *Hannah and Elizabeth,* of Boston, sometimes styled in the court records a "ship," brought forty-five passengers from Dartmouth, England, in 1679, and carried a ship's doctor, John Barton, who afterwards practiced medicine in Salem.

The fishing pink after a time became known as a "pinky" (*See* Fig. 177) and one form of the fishing pinky in common use along the northern shore of Massachusetts Bay during the seventeenth century and also well into the next century was the "Chebacco boat", so called because it was first built at Chebacco, now the town of Essex. Sometimes called "standing-room" boats, they were from ten to twelve tons burthen, had two masts, but no bowsprit. They were decked over with the exception of a space in the middle where were two rooms across the boat nearly to the sides, for the crew to stand in while fishing. In rough weather these rooms

PINKY AND
CHEBACCO
BOAT

*The buss was a two-masted vessel used by both English and Dutch in the herring fisheries. It usually was about sixty tons burden and at either end had a small shed or cabin, the one in the bow being used as a kitchen.

were covered with hatches.   The deck had no railing and the stern was sharp like the bow.   The last pink-sterned vessel built in Essex was one of thirty-five tons launched in 1844.

The fishing pinky and the Chebacco boat doubtless closely resembled the "two-masted boat," so-called, of the first half of the seventeenth century.   Another form of the two-masted THE KETCH boat was ketch-rigged and varied in size from the fishing ketch of small burthen to sea-going vessels of over one hundred tons.   The principal mast of the ketch was placed about amid-ship and the other, a shorter one, was close to the

BILANDER AND KETCH.
From an engraving in Steel's "Elements and Practice of Rigging and Seamanship,"
London, 1794.*

stern.   In the very early days these masts carried lateen sails but in the eighteenth century the larger mast had the yards and sails of the foremast of a ship and the smaller was rigged like the mizzenmast of a bark of the present time.   The bowsprit was long and on it were set two or three jibs.   Much of the eighteenth century trade with the

*In the upper left-hand corner of the "Price View of Boston" (see page 27 *post*), a ketch is depicted carrying a lateen sail on the shorter mast.

West Indies was carried on in vessels of this type. When John Turner, the Salem merchant, died in 1680, the inventory of his estate discloses that he owned: "the Keatch Blosome, 170li.; Keatch Prosperous, 120li.; Keatch John & Thomas, 100li.; Keatch Willing Mind, 90li.; 1/2 of ye Keatch with Mr. English, 190li.; 1/2 of ye pink Speedwell, 150li.; 3/8 of ye Keatch Society, 150li.; 3/8 of ye Keatch William & John, 100li.; 1/4 of ye Keatch Friendship, 65li.; 1/8 of ye Keatch Fraternyty, 40li.; a shallop at Marblehead, 50li.; 1/4 of ye sloop with John Hart, 40li.; a pleasure Boote, 8li.; 1/3 or 3/8 of the ship William & John, 500li." The inventory of his estate totalled £6,788li. 17s. 11d.

John Hull, the mint master, mentions in his diary, in 1658, that a Boston ketch "that went hence for England, was taken by a pirate of Ostend, and therein much estate lost."

In 1666, Jonathan Baulston, shipwright, of Boston, entered into an agreement with Samuel Legg, mariner, to sell one-half of a ketch, then on the stocks. It was forty-four feet keel upon a straight line, seventeen feet by the midship beam, nine feet deep in the hold from plank to plank, had a pink stern, a close steerage, "and a fall into the hold under the half deck." It was sold at the rate of £3. 8. 0. per ton.

The ketch *Margaret* of Salem, in 1697, carried a crew of four men and a boy. By that year Salem had lost, through captures by the French and Indians, some fifty-four of the sixty fishing ketches owned in that port. The captures were made along the Newfoundland coast and near Cape Sable, near the fishing grounds.

On Dec. 21, 1677, William Carr, shipwright, of Salisbury, Mass., signed an agreement to build for Robert Dutch, mariner, of Ipswich, a pink-stern ketch,—"a good & substantial Ketch to bee in length by ye keele thirty fower foot in breadth twelve foot by ye beame & six foot deep in ye hold to bee every way shipshapen. The said ketch to bee built with two inch white oake planke to ye upper wale & with inch & halfe white oake plank upward & to bee seiled fore & aft with ye like condiconed two inch planke: To lay her deck with good two inch pine plank: the fore Castle to bee raised twelue Inches & ye cabin abaft to bee raised two foot with scuttles & hatches sutable & to doe & compleat all builders worke to a cleat: to fitt her with all ye masts & yards & calke & lanche ye said ketch by ye last day of August next ensuing ye date hereof:" Carr was to be paid at the rate of £3. 5s. per ton and Dutch was to provide the ironwork.

The ketch is said to have sailed very fast before the wind. This rig disappeared from New England waters not long after the year 1800. Elias Hasket Derby, the Salem merchant, owned the ketch *John* in 1799.

Whale boats with sharp bow and stern were known before 1700. In December, 1748, a small boat "built in the fashion of a whale boat" was taken up in Boston harbor. Long before that date whaling was being carried on along the South Shore of the Bay and at Nantucket, by boats that made off from the shore whenever a whale was sighted.

BOATS

"A small Norway Yawl", painted red within, was stolen from Clark's wharf, Boston, in 1726. In 1754, a "Deal Yawl, with Masts, Oars and Sails" was advertised for sale in Boston and four years later a twenty-foot yawl "painted with white Flowers on a red ground" was stolen from the stern of a ship lying at anchor in the harbor. Not long after "a large Lugg Boat, having a short Fore-castle, with one of the Ribbins of her Bow split off, having no Oars on Board," was taken up below the Castle. In 1759, "a Shalloway, with her materials, as she now lays at Dyer's wharf," was advertised for sale at public vendue.

A ship's long boat, nineteen feet long, with "round Tuck, Painted Black and Yellow, a Swifter* round her, with her two Masts standing and sails bent," was stolen in Boston harbor and a reward of £3 offered. "A Moses-built boat, black Bottom and Soaped," was stolen in March, 1745 and in December a lapstreak boat with a 16 1/2 foot keel, went adrift. It was "painted in the Gunnel, the upper and lower streaks white, and the middle black, and her inside is red fore and aft and a black bottom." In 1749, "a Moses-built boat, about 14 or 15 Feet in length, her bottom pay'd with Pitch, and her sides with Turpentine and painted Red above her Wail" was cut away from the stern of the sloop *Sarah* lying at Long Wharf. Other advertisements reveal the fact that the Moses boat was flat-bottomed and built with a keel. In 1743, an advertisement describes "a small Long-Boat or Moses." Other types of boats appear in the advertisements. Some one is wanted to "go in a Mud-Boat for the summer season." "Distiller's boats" are mentioned, and a "Gondelo" is for sale in 1754. In 1758, two "gundelow" are offered for sale one of which could carry

*A strong rope encircling a boat to strengthen and defend her sides, usually fixed about a foot under the gunwale.

sixteen cords of wood. The gundelow has now practically disappeared from New England waters. All through the nineteenth century, and doubtless before, it was used to carry salt hay from distant banks to the landings were it could be loaded on carts and taken inland. It was propelled by means of long sweeps and a sail was also used, when possible.

English vessels of the earliest times carried lateen sails, a rig that still persists about the Mediterranean. As the centuries passed the larger vessels retained the lateen sail only on the mizzen mast. When William Burgis made his superb drawing of the shipping in Boston harbor, which was engraved in 1725, he pictured fourteen ships all of which are shown with a lateen sail on the mizzen. None of the sloops or schooners in the picture, of which there are many, carry the lateen yard. The mainsail is suspended by a gaff and fastened at the bottom to a boom. A century before, however, it is supposed that many of the smaller vessels in New England waters were lateen rigged. The long lateen yard was cumbersome and not easily worked in the small craft and after a time the progress of improvement evolved the fore-and-aft sail fastened to a boom. It undoubtedly was first used on the sloop. Its application to a two-masted rig was first made at Gloucester, Massachusetts, by Capt. Andrew Robinson, about the year 1713. In the diary of Dr. Moses Prince of Sandwich, under date of Sept. 12, 1752, he writes, during a visit to Gloucester:—

THE SCHOONER

"Went to see Capt. Robinson's lady. . . . This gentleman was the first contriver of schooners, and built the first of the sort about eight years since; and the use that is now made of them, being so much known, has convinced the world of their conveniency beyond other vessels and shows how mankind is obliged to this gentleman for this knowledge."

A more circumstantial account of the building of the first schooner appears in the diary of Cotton Tufts, M. D., of Weymouth, who visited Gloucester, Sept. 8, 1790 and wrote as follows:—

"I was informed (and commited the same to writing) that the kind of vessels called schooners derived their name from this circumstance; viz. Mr. Andrew Robinson of that place, having constructed a vessel which he masted and rigged as schooners are at this day, on her going off the stocks and passing into the water, a bystander cried out,

'Oh, how she scoons!' Robinson instantly replied, *'A scooner let her be!'* From which time, vessels thus masted and rigged have gone by the name of 'schooners'; before which, vessels of this description were not known in Europe or America. This account was confirmed to me by a great number of persons in Gloucester."

Babson, in his *History of Gloucester,* states that the earliest mention of the schooner that he was able to find in public records was an entry in the Gloucester town records in 1716 that a new "scooner" belonging to that town was cast away on the Isle of Sables. He further states that in the inventory, made in 1714, of the estate of John Parsons of Gloucester, who carried on the fishing business, a schooner is not listed among the vessels owned by him. Another man who died in 1714 and was interested in the fishing industry was John Wilson of Boston, a part owner in six different sloops "lying at Cape Anne," with no mention of a schooner in the inventory of his estate. The new rig, however, soon came into favor and ten years later was well known up and down the Atlantic coast and even in European ports.

The earliest mention of the schooner that we have been able to find in the *Boston News-Letter,* is in the Feb. 4/11, 1717 issue where mention is made that the "Schooner Ann" was outward bound for South Carolina. Usually the rig is not mentioned in the concise marine news of that time and doubtless other vessels so rigged may have entered and cleared without leaving a trace in the local news-sheet. Moreover, little attention was then paid to the coasting trade in the marine news and there probably the new rig made its first appearance. In the July 8/15, 1717 issue of the *News-Letter,* among the "entry-inwards" items, is the "Scooner Dolphin, Bartholomew Putnam, master, from Barbadoes." In the Nov. 10/17, 1717 issue is printed an account of piracy along the North Carolina coast and mention is made of the capture of two "scooners" one belonging to Boston, Snood, master, "and the other belonged to London," England.

In the spring of 1733, a fishing schooner was advertised for sale in the *News-Letter.* It had been built the previous year, had a twenty-nine foot keel, and had blocks "all with Lignum-vita sheves, and all her Blocks at Mast head strap'd with Iron. . . . She generally comes in twice a week."

In 1743, among the privateers fitted out by the Spaniards at Havana, was a "scooner haveing Top-sails and Cross-jack Yards aloft," with a crew of one hundred men.—*Boston News-Letter.*

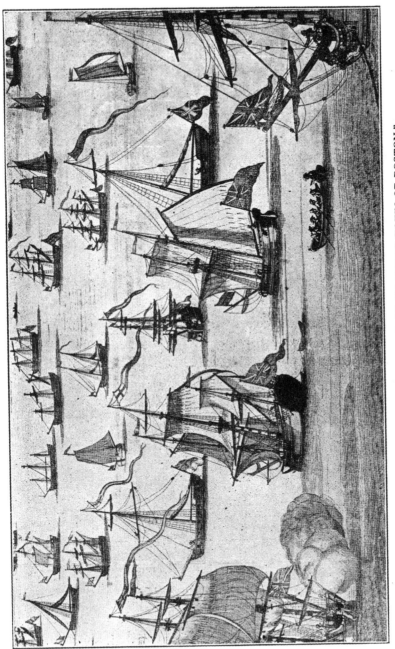

SECTION OF "A SOUTH EAST VIEW OF YE GREAT TOWN OF BOSTON."

Engraved by I. Harris after a drawing by William Burgis and published in 1725 by William Price.

In October, 1752, another fishing schooner was advertised for sale in the *Boston Gazette*. She then was on the stocks, "half planked, about 50 tons, with a streak at the floor head, and under the wale 2 & half Plank, and none but white oak plank and timber put into her. Trunnels to be drove in tarr and cork'd, named *The Boston's Beginning*, being the first to be off the Stocks, design'd for the Fishery; and is judg'd to be as good a Sailor as ever went out of Marblehead. . . . Miall Bacon of Boston, Shipwright."

The earliest pictorial representation of the schooner is found in William Price's *View of Boston*, engraved in 1725, where two schooners are shown at anchor in the harbor. (*See* page 27).

The bilander was a type of two masted sailing vessel that was not uncommon in New England waters during the first half of the eighteenth century. It was a kind of hoy and really was the fore-

BILANDER runner of the brig. The long mainsail yard on the mainmast of the bilander hung fore and aft and was inclined at an angle of about forty-five degrees. The foremost lower corner of this mainsail, called the "tack", was secured to a ring-bolt in the deck about the middle of the vessel and the aftermost of the sail, called the "sheet", was fastened to the taffrail. This gave much the effect of the lateen sail on the mizzenmast of the full rigged ship of that period.

A bilander owned in Boston, with its cargo of grain, was captured by a Spanish *barca longa* while going into Lisbon in the fall of 1740. In the *Boston News-Letter* of Mar. 11/18, 1742, is the following item of news:—"We hear from Rhode Island [i. e. Newport] that the Billander *Young Eagle* is ready to sail on a cruize against the Spaniards having on board 135 able seamen."

Much confusion exists concerning the various rigs of vessels. Most persons at all familiar with the sea readily recognize the ship, the bark or barque, and the schooner with from two to seven masts, but the older rigs,—those entirely obsolete and others just passing out are little known,—the ketch, the snow, the topsail schooner and the three forms of the brig.

"The American brig is a two-masted vessel entirely or partly square rigged. There are three classes of brigs; the full-rigged brig, the

THE BRIG brigantine and the hermaphrodite brig which is sometimes called the schooner-brig. All are square-rigged on the fore-mast (first mast) and in this respect they are all alike. The mainmast (second mast) is different in each of the three classes and it is on the mainmast that the disinctive points of difference are found.

"On the full-rigged brig both masts are made in three spars and both masts are square rigged. On the mainmast there is a standing gaff to which is rigged a small fore-and-aft sail. In other respects both masts are alike. (*See* Fig. 60)

"On the hermaphrodite brig, or half brig*, the mainmast is made in two spars and carries no yards; but it has a fore-and-aft, or hoist and lower mainsail and a gaff-topsail. The main-HERMAPHRO- mast is made and rigged like the mainmast of the DITE BRIG ordinary two-masted schooner; thus the hermaphrodite brig may be said to be half brig and half schooner and in some ports it is called a brig-schooner. (*See* Fig. 150)

"On the brigantine (*See* Fig. 89) the mainmast (second mast) is also made in two spars and has a fore-and-aft, or hoist and lower mainsail and is like the mainmast of the hermaphrodite brig; but the brigantine does not carry a gaff-topsail. In place BRIGANTINE of the gaff-topsail there are two and often three yards aloft on the mainmast over the large fore-and-aft mainsail. On these yards are carried a square main-topsail and, in the case of three main yards a main-top-gallantsail. There is generally no sail carried on the lower or main yard. These are small, light yards and are rigged and handled like the yards on the foremast. The brigantine might thus be considered as a compromise between the full-rigged brig and the hermaphrodite brig, and at a distance it very much resembles a full-rigged brig. The small main yards, or jack yards, as the yards carried on the brigantine's mainmast are often called, are in reality of but little use and are of more or less trouble and in many cases they have been taken off and a gaff-topsail rigged in their place. In such instances, of course, the brigantine becomes a hermaphrodite brig.

"The full-rigged brig and brigantine are entirely obsolete rigs and probably none of either class has been built in this country within the past sixty or seventy years. The hermaphrodite brig is also fast becoming obsolete and as late as 1916 but four brigs of this class are found in the American register.

*When the hermaphrodite brig carries one or more square topsails on the main-mast she is frequently called a "jackass brig."

"The topsail schooner (*See* Fig. 134) is a two-masted vessel having both masts made in two spars. The mainmast has a fore-and-aft mainsail and gaff-topsail the same as the ordinary two-masted schooner.

TOPSAIL
SCHOONER

The lower foremast is made a little shorter than the corresponding spar of the mainmast and the topmast a little longer. The foresail is a fore-and-aft sail and has no gaff-topsail; but aloft, over the foresail, there are two and sometimes three yards on which are carried a square fore-topsail and a fore-top-gallant-sail. There is usually no sail carried on the lower, or fore yard. The foremast and the sails carried on it are exactly like the mainmast of a brigantine."* Where there are square topsails on both masts the vessel is called a double-topsail schooner. (*See* Fig. 92)

The brig was a favorite rig in New England for deep-sea vessels during the eighteenth century and well into the next. She was more easily handled than the ship and less costly to fit. This rig was sometimes used on vessels of less than twenty-five tons and after the Revolution on vessels of considerable tonnage. The brig *Sally Brown,* of 426 tons, was built at Newburyport as late as 1865.

In 1756, Stephen Brown of Charlestown, advertised in the *Boston Gazette* for information concerning the brig *Providence,* 70 tons, "British built and very Moon shap'd, having a Horse Head," which sailed from Cadiz on Mar. 2, 1756, bound for Newfoundland and Boston. The brig was commanded by one Richard Murphey, "remarkable for Inebriety," and not having been heard from after sailing, Stephen Brown asked for information.

The snow was a form of brig-rigged vessel that was in frequent use before the nineteenth century (See Figs. 109, 287). It differed from

THE SNOW

the brig in that the try-sail was carried by a small mast set just abaft of the mainmast, its foot fixed in a block of wood or step and its head attached to the after part of the main-top. The "Snow or Barke Sea Flower, pinke sterned, about 20 Tons," was built in 1709 at Newbury. In 1737, a snow was built at Ipswich, "forty eight feet and half a foot Keel Streight Rabbet, Eighteen Inches of which not to be Tunaged for & nineteen feet Beam of Eight feet & nine Inches Deep in the hold between Plank & Ceiling, to be a Vessell with two Decks & to

*See "The Marine Room of the Peabody Museum of Salem," Salem, 1921.

be three feet & nine Inches between Decks, the rise of the Quarter Deck from the main Deck to be fifteen Inches & to be Ten feet & half a foot floor between Sir mark & Sirmark* the dead riseing to be Eight Inches, the running Plank to be all white oake & two Inches & one Quarter Thick, one Streek under the wale & one Streek next above the wale to be of three Inch white oake Plank, the wales to be four Inches thick & nine Inches in Breadth; the Gunnel wales to be six Inches Deep & three Inches Thick, the water way to be of two & half Inch white Oake Plank, the Other Decks to be of two Inch Pine Plank, the waterways upon the upper Decks to be of three Inch white Oake Plank, two streeks upon the main Deck to be of two & half Inch white Oake Plank," . . . †

The snow rig persisted well into the nineteenth century and was not then differentiated from the brig. Sometimes such small masts were set just abaft both masts. (*See* Fig. 176)

Richard Hollingsworth had a shipyard at Salem Neck as early as 1637 and in 1641 built "a prodigious ship of 300 Tons." Two years later a great ship was built at Gloucester by William Stevens, "an able shipwright" who had previously built in

THE SHIP   England many noble ships including the *Royal Merchant,* a ship of six hundred tons. In 1661, this William Stevens was building at Gloucester, for merchants in the Isle of Jersey, a ship of "68 foot long by ye keele, & 23 foot broad from outside to outside, & 9 & 1/2 feet in hold under ye beame, with two decks, forecastle, quarter deck and round house, ye deck from ye mainmast to ye forecastle, to be 5 foot high, with a fall at the forecastle 15 inches, and at ye mainmast to ye quarter deck of 6 inches; the great Cabbin to be 6 foot high." The local representative of the foreign owners was "to find all Iron work carved work & joiners in time soe yt ye work be not hindered," and Stevens was to paid at the rate of £3. 5. 0 per ton.

Shipbuilding has been carried on at some time or other at almost every seacoast town in New England as well as in many other towns reached by navigable streams. Not infrequently vessels of considerable size were built near the homes of their builders and when completed were loaded on wheels or rollers and hauled to a suitable

*Surmark—the position of the rib and fore parts of the wales which are marked on the timbers.

†Notarial records at the Essex County Court House, Salem.

launching place, The largest vessel ever built in the town of Rowley was the *Country's Wonder,* of ninety tons, the keel of which was layed on Rowley Common, and when completed this vessel was hauled to the river, over a mile and a half distant, by more than a hundred yoke of oxen.

In October, 1732, "a stately Mast Ship" was launched at Mr Clark's shipyard at the North End of Boston, an abundance of spectators being present. The *Boston News-Letter* states that it was thought to be the largest ship ever built in the Province "being above 500 Tuns."

The ship is usually of larger size than most other sailing vessels and has three masts each of which is composed of a lower mast, a topmast, a top-gallantmast and sometimes, formerly, a royal mast. The rig of the ship is well known to all interested in the sea and every detail is shown in the numerous illustrations that follow. The same cannot be said of the fittings of ships, especially as they must have varied somewhat at different periods. For example, the question has recently been asked: "When did the capstan first come into use in the merchant service?" From incidental allusion and from old inventories and commercial papers it is possible to reconstruct a fair idea of the old equipment and the following inventory, found in some old notarial records at the Essex County Court House, at Salem, is of considerable interest:

SHIP FITTINGS

"Inventory of Ship Providence Galley about Ninety Tunns with most of her Standing Rigging with her masts & yards Lying Mored In Salem Harbour Near ye Southfield. To a sheet cable & a sheet anchor, a small Bower Cable & ditto anchor, a Harser & a small anchor, Eight great Gunns & Gun tacks, to 81 Iron round shot, 25 Double headed ditto, to an Iron Hatch Barr & 2 Scuttle Barrs, three poop lights, to Three Top armour, Two Quart'r Cloths,* an English Jack & pennant, three Goose Necks for ye Lanthorns, to a mainsail, a maintopsail, a foresail & foretopsail, to a Mizen sail & Mizen Topsail, a spritsail & spritsail topsail, two Top Gallant sails, two old Stay sails, one old foresail, to some of ye standing riging & ye running being 34 Quoiles, to 6 parrells & parrell roapes, 4 parcel of Strapt blocks & other Blocks & dead Eyes, 2 Buoy roapes, 2 catt blocks, a Tackle Hooke, an Iron Stirrup, a L : 3, 2 Tarpolines, Twelve Water Caske, about 7li. Spun yarne, a Bedstead, a Cabin bell, a looking glass, a pinnace & 3 oars, 14 Irons for boats awning, a fine wrought

*Long pieces of painted canvas fastened along the rail of the quarter deck to keep out the spray.

Awning cloth for ye boat and a Carpett, 2 Sails for Pinnace. Stuff curtains for ye boat, two compasses, a half Watch Glass, two Half Hour Glasses, a frying pan, a spitt, two iron potts, a pr. pot Hooks, a fork, an ax, a handsaw, a small Hammer, an adz, two augers, a drawing knife, to a Caulking Mallet, 4 Marling Spicks, 3 shod shouels, two hand pumps, three lanthorns, six Iron Scrapers, a hand lead and line, a Deep sea Lead & line, a Bilbo bolt, a half minute glass, a grindstone, a Tin dripping pan, 2 Canns, a ladle, a wooden platter, 3 padlocks, a fishing gig, a fish Hook, a Copper Sauce panne, a parcel of old nails & Staples, six muskets, 4 Catouch boxes, Three Brass Blunderbusses, 1 Iron Ditto, Six Cutlasses, three ladles & worms, three spring Staues, three roape ditto, four Crab Handspecks, a parcell of match. Two Gunne Iron Crows, a Gunne Mallet, Two formers, 3 small Tin Pots, a parcell of small Hooks & lins pins, a wormer, & Scourer for small arms, nine Catridge Cases, Two Pump Speers & pump breaks, 2 Setts boxes, a Pump hook, a parcell of priming Irons wire, &c. for great gunns, 1 file & pr Nippers, Ships Canvas & awning cloth, six cane chairs, a Pewter Bason, 6 pewter Plates, another ax, 1 pr small Stillairds, 1 pr bed Window Curtains, about 3 Tunn limestones on board ye ship." Salem, March 16, 1703/4.

The bark has three masts and is square-rigged like a ship on her fore and mainmast, but the mizzenmast carries no topsail yards the topsail being hung by a gaff. (*See* Fig. 21) A

THE BARK jackass-bark has no cross-trees and no tops or platforms over the heads of the lower masts (*See* Fig. 36). The barkentine is square-rigged on the foremast with fore-and-aft sails on the other masts (*See* Fig. 153).

In the early days small ships were frequently called barks. The bark rig did not come into general use in New England until after 1800. The bark *Harriet and Eliza,* 187 tons, was built at Haverhill in 1793. Only four bark-rigged vessels were built on the Merrimack river previous to 1831.

At how early a date vessels were painted is not known. Manuscripts, illuminated centuries before the art of printing was discovered, preserve drawings of shipping indicating that the hulls of vessels were painted—at least in the minds of the illumin-

PAINT ON ators. It is reasonable to suppose, however, that VESSELS ship-builders at an early date would devise some means of preserving the surface of the hulls of vessels from decay brought about by exposure to the action of salt water. Pitch and a composition of resin and tallow were used on ship's bot-

toms until after 1760 when copper was first used for sheathing.*
Various experiments had previously been made including the trial of
an outside sheathing of elm boards and the use of sheet lead.   The
earliest mention of paint that we have found in connection with a
New England vessel is in 1692.   In an account of provisions supplied
and repairs made that year on the ship *Scanderberg,* William Hall,
master, of Boston, while on a voyage to Providence (the Bahamas)
for salt, is the following item: "painting ye vessel £5."   This docu-
ment is preserved in the *Massachusetts Archives,* Vol. 61, leaf 550.
There is also a charge for "Sugar Plums and Oatmeal 16/."

The Boston newspapers preserve scraps of information on the subject.   A wreck of a new square-sterned vessel seen near Georges bank
in April, 1705, was painted yellow and had considerable carved work
on her stern; and in July of the same year the wreck of a new ship
was found on Montenicus rocks, having a white bottom and all her
carved work painted yellow.   In 1707, a fishing ketch saw a small
new ship painted red, with "a low snug head and low forward,"
standing out of Barnstable Bay.   " 'Tis feared to be a Rogue† by his
working," continues the account.   The wreck of a sloop seen off Nantucket in December, 1747, had a white bottom, blue stern and hants
and the four cabin windows had a white moulding around them.   In
1754, a wreck of about 400 tons burden was reported off the Capes
of the Chesapeake, that "had clean Turpentine sides."   In 1756, a
vessel arriving at New York reported passing a wreck.   "Two of her
masts had parted, and were alongside, which were painted yellow,
with some black streaks like mouldings round them."   A dismasted
sloop of eighty tons found at sea near the Isles of Sables, in June,
1756, was "painted blue on her stern, and had Blue Hants, yellow
streaks, and half-moon hinges on her Cabbin Windows."   In the fall
of the next year a dismasted sloop was sighted off the Capes of the
Chesapeake.   "Her Quarters were painted with a dirty Blue, with a
White Scrowl."   About the same time a wrecked schooner was
sighted, newly sheathed, the upper streak was yellow, with a rise aft
which took in her mainmast and pumps, "and had a Sea-Horse Head."
The wreck of a new sloop sighted off New York harbor in 1761, had

*An old formula for "paying" a vessel's bottom was one part tallow, one part
brimstone and three parts resin.   One hundred and forty pounds would be used
for a vessel of one hundred and forty tons.

†A pirate.

her stern and quarters painted green. A topsail schooner from Casco Bay, Maine, that was boarded by a tide surveyor below Philadelphia, in February, 1775, was "deep waisted, with two small ports on each side of the waist, brown bottom and her quarters painted light blue."

"Painter's colors" were advertised in the *Boston News-Letter,* as early as March, 1711. "All Sorts of Colours ground in Oyle, fit for Painting, by Wholesale or Retail" were advertised in 1724. John Merritt who kept a shop in King's Street, Boston, in 1738, advertised for sale "White lead, Red lead, Spanish white, Spanish brown, Spruce yellow, Fine Smalts (3 Sorts), Vermilian Red, Indian Red, Ruddle, Terraumber, Carmine and other Fine Colours (Sixteen in Number) for Oyl or Water." He also sold "Linseed Oyl, Nut Oyl, Turpentine Oyl, Varnish." Lampblack was available and several red and yellow earths had been found that were used for painting, while hog's bristles were to be had everywhere. Doubtless more or less of this paint was used in house painting but much must have been used on vessels and boats. The carved figureheads carried by all ships must have been protected and also rendered more realistic by the use of paint, and this was also true of the "gingerbread work" about the cabin windows and the stern. In war ships, below decks, the gun carriages and all the surfaces were painted a dull red which prevented human blood, spattered about during a battle, from becoming too conspicuous.

The ship Sooloo, of 440 tons, built at Salem in 1840, had an unpainted hull (*See* Fig. 262), and doubtless many other vessels were sent to sea with "turpentine sides", long after the use of paint became common.

Very little is known at the present time concerning life on board ship in the early times and especially as to the accommodations provided for passengers. On the vessels that brought over emigrants in any number, the living conditions during the ACCOMMODATIONS voyage must have been well-nigh intolerable beFOR PASSENGERS cause of crowding many people into limited space and also lack of the necessary conveniences of life and the meagre equipment. During the period of the German emigration, and that from northern Ireland in the mid-eighteenth century, there was frequently a high mortality during the voyage and sometimes when it was of unusual length the supply of food and water ran short and there was terrible suffering. Doubtless some attempt was made to separate the sexes and the families but cases are found in the court records from time to time in which deposition or testimony clearly show that living conditions on shipboard in the early days were decidedly of a miscellaneous character. It is known that sometimes in the more regular passenger service the main cabin was parted off at night by means of curtains. Small cabins also were built and especially in the larger ships. It is impossible to imagine that it could be otherwise, for officials and their wives were frequently crossing the ocean, and Boston shopkeepers, London merchants and speculators were constantly going abroad to buy or to sell.

The captain's cabin had its steward and there the food and service undoubtedly were better than that provided forward where all slept in canvas hammocks slung from hooks in the deck timbers overhead and served themselves from the galley. The foul odors below deck and the unsanitary conditions are part of the lore of the sea. "Ship feaver" was well known to all physicians practicing in seaport towns. At the time of the Revolution well ventilated toilet accommodations were provided for the crew in the bow of the larger vessls, usually on the berth deck.*

In those days the cooking on shore was done in an open fireplace. So, too, on ship board there was provided an open "hearth" made of cast iron and weighing from four to eight hundred pounds. This was fastened to the deck and its "chimney" was screened by a "smoke sail." The chimney was sometimes made of soapstone but usually it was cast iron. Advertisements or references to ship's "hearths" and to "cabin stoves" may be frequently noted in the newspapers of the time. In 1720, the appurtenances of the ship *Thomas and Benjamin,* wrecked on the coast of South Carolina, were brought to Boston and sold at vendue. Included were "one Iron Hearth weighing about 7 C. weight, one large double Copper Furnace belonging to it. Fender, Shovel and Tongs belonging to Cabin Stove," etc. Hearths were used in small vessels as well as on the larger ones, for fire broke out on a small sloop lying at Long Wharf, Boston, in November, 1731, "occasioned thro' some defect in the Hearth." In the summer of 1730, a new ship lying at anchor in Boston harbor was struck by lightning which "melted the top of the iron spindle of the vane of the mainmast" and passing through the long boat, which lay on the deck,

*Middlebrook—*The Connecticut Ship "Defence,"* Hartford, 1922.

VIEW OF CASTLE WILLIAM, BOSTON HARBOR, IN 1729
AND A SHIP OF THE PERIOD.

From the only known copy of an engraving probably by John Harris after a drawing
by William Burgis published Aug. 11, 1729 by William Price of Boston.

killed two men and injured two others as "they were eating together off the Hen-Coop, near the Main Mast."

Travelers to America or abroad, in their printed accounts of travel, seldom comment at length on the voyage and rarely mention their quarters on board ship. One description, however, has come to our attention,—that of a New Englander going abroad in 1760,—which merits attention.

Jacob Bailey, a native of Rowley, Mass., and a graduate of Harvard College, having prepared for the ministry and been licensed to preach, determined to obtain orders in the Church of England and so, through the intervention of friends, took passage from Boston for London in the *Hind,* a twenty-gun ship, which sailed from Nantasket Roads, in company with six other vessels, on Jan. 19, 1760. Mr. Bailey kept a diary of the voyage and his description of the accommodations which the ship supplied, the life on board, and the men with whom he was brought in contact, is a surprisingly vivid picture of strange and uncouth conditions attending passenger service to England in the mid-century. The ship lay at anchor in the harbor and Mr. Bailey went out to her in a small boat.

"The wind was blowing strong and it was some time before we could get on board ship. At length, with difficulty, I clambered up the side and found myself in the midst of a most horrid confusion. The deck was crowded full of men, and the boatswain's shrill whistle, with the swearing and hallooing of the petty officers, almost stunned my ears. I could find no retreat from this dismal hubbub, but was obliged to continue jostling among the crowd above an hour before I could find anybody at leisure to direct me. At last, Mr Letterman, the Captain's steward, an honest Prussian, perceiving my disorder, introduced me through the steerage to the lieutenant. I found him sitting in the great cabin. He appeared to be a young man, scarce twenty years of age, and had in his countenance some indications of mildness. Upon my entrance he assumed a most important look and with a big voice demanded to know my request. I informed him that I was a passenger on board the Hind, by permission of Capt. Bond, and desired that he would be civil enough to direct me to the place of my destination. He replied in this laconic style: 'Sir, I will take care to speak to one of my mates.' This was all the notice, at present. But happily, on my return from the cabin, I found my chest and bedding carefully stowed away in the steerage. In the mean time the ship was unmoored and we fell gently down to Nantasket. . . .

"I observed a young gentleman walking at a distance, with a pensive air in his countenance. Coming near him, in a courteous manner he invited me down between decks to a place he called his berth. I thanked him for his kindness and readily followed him down a ladder into a dark and dismal region, where the fumes of pitch, bilge water, and other kinds of nastiness almost suffocated me in a minute. We had not proceeded far before we entered a small appartment, hung round with damp and greasy canvas, which made, on every hand, a most gloomy and frightful appearance. In the middle stood a table of pine, varnished over with nasty slime, furnished with a bottle of rum and an old tin mug with a hundred and fifty bruises and several holes, through which the liquor poured in as many streams. This was quickly filled with toddy and as speedily emptied by two or three companions who presently joined us in this doleful retreat. Not all the scenes of horror about us could afford me much dismay till I received the news that this detestable appartment was allotted by the captain to be the place of my habitation during the voyage!

"Our company continually increased, when the most shocking oaths and curses resounded from every corner, some loading their neighbors with bitter execrations, while others uttered imprecations too awful to be recorded. The persons present were: first, the captain's clerk, the young fellow who gave me the invitation. I found him a person of considerable reading and observation who had fled his native country on account of a young lady to whom he was engaged. Second, was one John Tuzz, a midshipman and one of my messmates, a good-natured, honest fellow, apt to blunder in his conversation and given to extravagant profaneness. Third, one Butler, a minister's son, who lived near Worcester, in England. He was a descendant from Butler, the author of Hudibras, and appeared to be a man of fine sense and considerable breeding, yet, upon occasion, was extremely profane and immodest, yet nobody seemed a greater admirer of delicacy in women than himself. My fourth companion was one Spears, one of the mates, a most obliging ingenious young gentleman who was most tender of me in my cruel sickness. Fifth: one of our company this evening was the carpenter of the ship who looked like a country farmer, drank excessively, swore roundly and talked extravagantly. Sixth: was one Shephard, an Irish midshipman, the greatest champion of profaneness that ever fell under my notice. I scarce ever knew him to open his mouth without roaring out a tumultuous volley of stormy oaths and imprecations. After we had passed away an hour or two together, Mr. Lisle, the lieutenant of marines, joined our company. He was about fifty years of age, of gigantic stature, and quickly distinguished himself by the quantities of liquor he poured down his throat. He also was very profane.

"About nine o'clock the company began to think of supper, when a boy was called into the room. Nothing in human shape did I ever see before so loathsome and nasty. He had on his body a fragment only of a check shirt, his bosom was all naked and greasy, over his shoulders hung a bundle of woolen rags which reached in strings almost down to his feet, and the whole composition was curiously adorned with little shining animals. The boy no sooner made his appearance than one of our society accosted him in this gentle language: 'Go, you ———— rascal, and see whether lobscouse is ready.' Upon this the fellow began to mutter and scratch his head, but after two or three hearty curses, went for the galley and presently returned with an elegant dish which he placed on the table. It was a composition of beef and onions, bred and potatoes, minced and stewed together, then served up with its broth in a wooden tub, the half of a quarter cask. The table was furnished with two pewter plates, the half of one was melten away, and the other, full of holes, was more weather-beaten than the sides of the ship; one knife with a bone handle, one fork with a broken tine, half a metal spoon and another, taken at Quebec, with part of the bowl cut off. When supper was ended, the company continued their exercise of drinking, swearing and carousing, till half an hour after two, when some of these obliging gentlemen made a motion for my taking some repose. Accordingly, a row of greasy canvas bags, hanging overhead by the beams, were unlashed. Into one of them it was proposed that I should get, in order to sleep, but it was with the utmost difficulty I prevented myself from falling over on the other side. . . .

"The next day, towards evening, several passengers came on board, viz.: Mr Barons, late Collector, Major Grant, Mr Barons' footman, and Mrs. Cruthers, the purser's wife, a native of New England. After some considerable dispute, I had my lodgings fixed in Mr Pearson's berth, where Master Robant, Mr Barons' man, and I agreed to lie together in one large hammock."

Such were the accomodations of the petty officers' mess on board a twenty-gun ship of 1760 in the New England service.

Jacob Bailey crossed the Atlantic in a heavily armed ship, in every sense a war vessel. At the same time, as before and after, there were packet ships making voyages at regular intervals and bringing from England the great variety of manufactured products required by a Province that was growing in wealth. These packet ships also carried passengers and sailing on somewhat regular schedules depended upon a profit made from freight and passage money rather than from cargoes shipped by their owners. In 1762, a line of "pacquet sloops" was plying weekly between Newport, R. I. and New York, "to transport Passengers and merchandize . . . Every Cabin Passenger, one Pistole, Steerage ditto, Two Dollars. . . . a Two Wheel Carriage, one Pistole; a Horse or Cow, one Pistole. All Baggage as Customary."

Letters were delivered at the Post Office at four pence each. The freight on cask goods was thirty-two shillings a ton; bar iron was sixteen shillings a ton; rum, eight shillings a hogshead; and butter, nine pence a firkin. After the War of 1812 several lines of packet ships were established sailing from Boston and New York, making quick passages and furnishing comfortable cabin accommodations for passengers. In 1837, the cabin passage from New York to Liverpool cost $140. which included "provisions, wines, beds, etc. Each ship has a separate cabin for ladies and each stateroom, in the respective cabins, will accommodate two passengers."*

Not long after this there came a demand for larger and swifter sailing vessels which resulted in the clipper-ship, that wonder of marine architecture. The clipper-ship undoubtedly was a development of the type of vessel built about the Chesapeake Bay not long after the year 1800, that was usually schooner-rigged and carried much canvas. The "Baltimore clippers," (See Fig.

CLIPPER- 134) as they came to be known, were built with
SHIPS sharp ends, the bow cutting through the waves instead of bluntly striking them. The slender stern, with its deep under-cutting, was a modification of earlier lines that facilitated the passage of the hull through the water. It slid cleanly through the dead-water behind the vessel with a minimum of resistance. The hull of the clipper-ship was also lengthened to an unheard-of extent in proportion to its width. The *Flying Cloud* (See Fig. 97) built at East Boston in 1851 by Donald McKay, measured 229 feet in length on the deck and only forty feet and eight inches in breadth. It is small wonder that on her first voyage she logged 1256 miles in four consecutive days and made one day's run of 374 miles. The word clipper, as applied to a fast vessel, is supposed to have originated in the Pennsylvania-German word *Klepper,* meaning a fast horse.

The clipper-ship rapidly came into prominence with the great demand for speedy transportation incidental to the California gold discovery. This type of vessel was also largely employed in the China tea trade for unlike wine, which is improved by the long sea voyage, tea quickly loses it delicate flavor and quality when kept in the ship's hold. Much has been written concerning the remarkable voyages made by these clippers and one volume—"The Clipper Ship Era," has

*McCullough's Commercial Dictionary, 1839.

become a classic in marine literature. The very recent death of its author, Capt. Arthur H. Clark, deprives us of a further contribution on this subject, which Captain Clark had in preparation for the present volume, embodying later results of his painstaking investigations.

The yacht is of Dutch origin, the "word in the seventeenth century signifying a transport for royalty or some individual of distinguished rank." At that time it was usually rigged with two masts but with no headsails. The stern was high and decorated EARLY with much carving and gilt. When Charles II was YACHTS restored to the throne in 1660 he came over from Holland in a Dutch yacht and the type of vessel soon became popular in England. Royal yachts were commonly rigged as ketches. In 1769, when Falconer published his *Marine Dictionary,* he noted that "private pleasure-vessels when sufficiently large for a sea-voyage, are also termed yachts."

The sloop *Jefferson,* built in Salem in 1801, for George Crowinshield, is often referred to as the first pleasure yacht in America. She was thirty-five feet long, of twenty-two tons burthen, and at one time was rigged as a schooner. *Cleopatra's Barge (See* Fig. 47), launched in 1816 and built for the same owner, was the first American yacht of note and the first to cross the Atlantic. It appears, however, that Sir William Pepperrell, Bart., of Kittery, Maine, died possessed of a pleasure yacht, the "Molly Yatch, being a fine schooner almost new, burthen about 100 Tons," which was advertised to be sold in the Dec. 3, 1759 issue of the *Boston Gazette.* The Royal Governors of the Province of New York also were using a yacht before 1750 whenever business required a journey up the Hudson river and there are several references to yachts owned by Col. Lewis Monis and others, in New York, from 1717 to 1746.* Nathaniel Hawthorne while visiting Thomaston, Maine, in 1837, commented on the condition of the estate formerly owned by General Knox and wrote in his Note Book:—"On the banks of the river, where he intended to have one wharf for his his own West India vessels and yacht, there are two wharves, with stores and a lime-kiln." Hawthorne states that the time was forty years before, *i. e.* in 1797.†

Very little appears to have been written upon the nautical instruments used on the early ships, although it is frequently asked "What

*Clark, History of Yachting, page 136.
†Hawthorne, American Notes, Aug. 12, 1837.

SIXTEENTH CENTURY ARABIAN ASTROLABE
8 1-2 inches in diameter. From Peabody Museum, Salem.

nautical instruments did Columbus use and what were used on the *Mayflower?*" And coming down to comparatively recent times, "What instruments were available and were actually used on the vessels during the commercial-marine activities following the American Revolution and up to the time of the appearance of steamships?"

NAUTICAL
INSTRUMENTS

These questions are often asked, not only by landsmen but by sea-faring men as well. The shipmaster of today uses instruments so different from those of Colonial times, or even of the earlier years of the nineteenth century, that unless he has a penchant for research he knows nothing about the earlier ones and certainly not how to use them if by chance they come to his notice. Holding in his hand a Davis quadrant, the skilful navigator of Salem's last square-rigger, the ship *Mindoro,* which passed out of service in 1897, said: "I have no idea how to use it and I do not believe that there is a shipmaster sailing out of Boston today who does." The Davis quadrant was in common use all through the eighteenth century and probably later. It is figured and explained in a book on navigation as late as 1796. The English navigator, John Davis, the inventor of this quadrant, in his "Seaman's Secrets," printed in 1594, gives a list of instruments which should be taken on ships, but it is to be feared few vessels carried them all or that owners were able to provide them. It included, — sea-compass, cross-staff, chart, quadrant, astrolabe, instrument to test compass variation, horizontal plane sphere, and paradoxical compass.

The astrolabe was devised during the first millennium and Arabian astronomers had perfected it as early as the year 700. It is really the basis of all future instruments of its class, — cross-staff, quadrant, sextant. Some of the most beautiful astrolabes preserved in museums are those made for Persian astronomers in the sixteenth and seventeenth centuries. If Columbus had one it probably was the form devised by Martin Behaim which had been adapted for use at sea about the year 1480. Observations with the astrolabe required three persons, one to hold the instrument plumb by the ring, another to sight the sun and adjust the arm, and the third to read the scale. With these difficulties observations were, of course, far from accurate, but approximate time and latitude could be obtained. Another device was the ring-dial, or universal ring-dial as the old works on navigation called

ASTROLABE

it. This differed from the astrolabe by having adjustable rings with the hours and scales engraved upon them. Ring dials were in use in New England and as late as 1716 were advertised for sale in Boston.

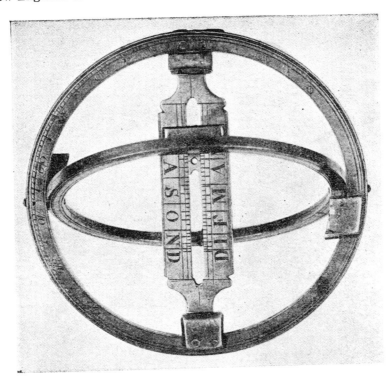

UNIVERSAL RING-DIAL.
Diameter 3 1-2 inches. Handle missing. Owned by Mr. Parker Kemble.

The cross-staff, or fore-staff, consisted of a four-square rod of hard wood, thirty-six inches long with four cross pieces made to slide upon it at right angles. These were of different lengths and were known as the ten, thirty, sixty and ninety cross, and were used singly upon the staff according to the height of the sun or star at the time of the observation. By sliding the cross-piece up or down and sighting from the end of the staff until the sun was seen at one end of the cross and the horizon at the other, the figure at the

CROSS-STAFF
OR
FORE-STAFF

junction of the cross and staff on the side to which that particular cross belonged indicated the sun's altitude and from this the latitude was obtained. Governor Winthrop, while on his voyage to New England, records in his *Journal,* on April 15, 1630 :—"at noon our captain made observation by the cross-staff, and found we were in forty-seven degrees thirty-seven minutes north latitude."

SEVENTEENTH CENTURY
MARINER USING A
CROSS-STAFF
From Seller's "Practical
Navigation," London, 1676.

SEVENTEENTH CENTURY
MARINER USING DAVIS'
QUADRANT
From Seller's "Practical
Navigation," London, 1676.

Based on this instrument, by laying out the circle on a table, John Davis the explorer, devised his quadrant in 1586. At first the ob-

QUADRANT

server used it by facing the sun, as the cross-staff had been used, but a better form was made later where the observer had the sun at his back. This instrument has been called by sailors "jackass quadrant" and, supposedly from its shape, "hog-yoke." In early books on navigation it is called "sea-quadrant," and it was also known as a "back-staff," in distinction from the "fore-staff" which continued in use for many years after Davis invented the quadrant. The earlier form used by the observer standing back to the sun had a solid "shade vane" which slid along the smaller arc of the instrument. By adjusting this a little short of the supposed altitude of the sun and sighting the horizon through the minute hole in the "sight vane" until it was seen through the "horizon vane" at the apex of the instrument, and then gradually moving the "sight vane" along the larger arc until the shadow of the "shade vane" met the horizon line, the sum of the degrees, on the two scales indicated the sun's altitude. This was really the second form of the Davis quadrant. In the third form, the solid "shade vane" was replaced by one with a low-power lens inserted in it arranged to focus on the "horizon vane," thus approaching the idea of the reflected sun in the Hadley quadrant and the sextant. A most interesting instrument, half-way between

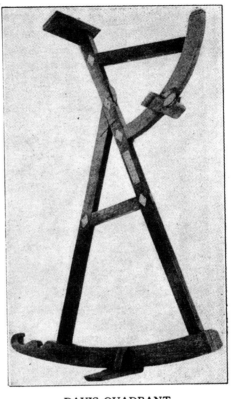

DAVIS QUADRANT.
"Made by William Williams in King St. Boston." An ivory plate has "Malachi Allen 1768." Mahogany, 24 inches long, convex glass in the shade vane; fine example of cabinet work. In Peabody Museum, Salem.

a cross-staff and the Davis quadrant, is illustrated in Seller's book on navigation published in 1676. He calls it a "Plough." Above, it has the small arc of the Davis quadrant with the sliding rod of the cross-staff below.

The Davis quadrants were usually made of ebony, rosewood, or other dark woods, with boxwood scale-arcs and could be made by expert wood-workers. The numerous examples preserved attest the skill of

NOCTURNAL

Inscribed "Nath'll Viall 1724." Boxwood, arm seven inches from centre to tip. In Peabody Museum, Salem.

the old cabinet-makers, for they are never warped or twisted while their jointing is a Chinese puzzle.

Whether the compass was independently invented in Europe or was borrowed from the Chinese is uncertain. Old marine compasses were set in gimbals. The magnet was a thin bar attached, usually with sealing wax, to the under side of the compass card, the whole mounted in a thin bowl of turned wood. These were the compasses of the eighteenth century. There is one in the Salem Marine Museum inscribed,—"Benjamin King Salem in New England," with the date "1770" cut in the box; another has the mark of Benjamin King, 1790. A surveyor's compass, wooden throughout, including wooden sights, is inscribed,—"Made by James Halsey* near ye draw bridge Boston." The liquid compass, first suggested by Francis Crow in 1813 and improved by E. S. Ritchie of Boston, has largely displaced the older devices.

The "nocturnal," used at night, as its name signifies, appeared at an early date, exactly when, it does not seem possible to say. By adjusting the movable discs to the date on the scale for the day of the month, sighting the north star through the hole in the center and then bringing the arm against the "guard stars," the hour was indicated with reasonable accuracy. "A Fore-staff and Nocturnal" were sold at public vendue in Boston, Sept. 5, 1723. Good pictures and descriptions of the nocturnal may be found in old books on navigation.

*James Halsey, jun., of Boston, was making Hadley quadrants or octants in 1738.

HADLEY QUADRANTS (OCTANTS) IN PEABODY MUSEUM, SALEM

1. "Made by John Dupee 1755 for Patrick Montgomerie." All wood, ebony, arm 22 inches long.

2. "Made by Ino. Gilbert on Tower Hill London for Hector Orr Augt. 6, 1768." Ebony, arm 20 inches long.

3. "Norie & Co. London." Ebony and brass, *ca.* 1840, arm 11 3-4 inches, telescopic eyepieces, used by Capt. John Hod ges.

4. "Spencer Browning and Rust London." Ebony frame, brass arm 17 inches, ivory scale, pencil inserted in cross piece, *ca.* 1800, used by Capt. Henry King.

5. "J: Urings London." All brass, arm 20 inches, back sight broken off, *ca.* 1780, rare.

In 1730, John Hadley in England and Thomas Godfrey in Philadelphia, independently invented the octant, known for nearly two hundred years as Hadley's quadrant.   Both Hadley and Godfrey received awards for their devices.   Although called quadrant in this country it is generally known elsewhere as octant, which is the better name, for the instrument represents but one eighth of the circle.   By the principle of reflection, however, it covers ninety degrees and the scale is so marked.   The Davis quadrant with its two arcs does represent one fourth of the circle and for that instrument the name is correct.

The Hadley was a great improvement over the Davis quadrant and other older devices for finding latitude.   By moving the arm the sun is reflected by the mirror at the apex and "brought down" to the horizon line and the eye is protected by colored glasses of various degrees of density through which the sun's rays pass.   The Hadley quadrant is still used in its modern form with telescopic eye-pieces.   Very moderately priced quadrants are made without the telescope, for use on fishing vessels.

The early Hadley quadrants were huge affairs made of wood with an arm twenty-four inches in length.   Today they are more generally of metal with arms from ten to twelve inches.   Using the sextent or Hadley quadrant the observer stands facing the sun, but old Hadley quadrants were made with a "back sight" so that they could be used like the Davis quadrant, thus making two independent observations the average of which would ensure greater accuracy.

"Hadley's New Invented Quadrant or Octant, the best and exactest Instrument for taking the Latitude or other altitudes at sea, as ever yet Invented, made and sold by Joseph Halsey, jun." is advertised in the *Boston Gazette*, Sept. 18/25, 1738.

"Adams' new fashion Quadrant and other Seamen's Instruments" were advertised for sale in December, 1756, at William Winters Vendue Room, Boston.

The sextant, one-sixth of the circle and by reflection one-third, is a more accurate instrument and also may be used to make lunar observations to obtain longitude, a complicated and difficult matter.   It was devised about 1757 and as now made is framed

SEXTANT   wholly of metal.   To prevent corrosion, the scale, which is minutely divided and has a "vernier" with a magnifying glass to show divisions of minutes, is made of gold or platinum in the best instruments.   A half-circle has been devised and is exceedingly rare. An example in the Salem collection was made before 1818. A curious double-jointed dividers accompanied it and the entry in the museum catalog reads,—"used to correct a lunar observation for longitude." A full "circle of reflection" is also used. This is a beautiful instrument and is not often met with in collections or in use. All of these instruments are similar in character and may be traced, as previously stated, to the ancestral astrolabe.

To obtain the ship's latitude with comparatively good results was an easy matter with the quadrant and its fore-runners, but the great problem for centuries was how to find the longitude, now universally and quickly obtained by the chronometer and simple observations in the morning or at noon. Spring clocks and watches appeared about 1530 but they were unreliable and of no use on long voyages. Large sand glasses, similar to those used in old Colonial churches, called "sea-clocks" and fitted with eyes or grommets above and below so that the glass might swing from a hook and be readily turned, were used on ships and so conservative is the British mind that some were in use on British naval vessels as late as 1828 and one authority states as late as 1839. Greenwich Observatory was established in 1675 and a Royal Commission was soon appointed with authority to award prizes for important inventions in aid of navigation. A prize of £20,000 was finally offered for a time-keeper that should meet certain requirements which practically meant absolute accuracy. In 1767, John Harrison produced the chronometer, based on the principle of an invention of 1735, and eventually he received the reward. Chronometers were so expensive and so hard to obtain that few New England ships had them until more than a half a century later. They were advertised for sale in 1817, by Thomas Biggs of Philadelphia. Other devices were tried to obtain longitude by lunar observations and by Jupiter's satellites, but these observations were too difficult to be of practical use. Today, fine watches serve for short trips and chronometers are carried by nearly all vessels making long voyages.

That so important an instrument as a telescope or spy-glass is rarely mentioned in books on navigation or in sea journals seems strange and it is exceedingly difficult to obtain early information of any being taken to sea. Telescopes did not become of practical use, even if the principle had been known, until they were made in Holland in 1608. It is at least certain that Columbus did not have one and probably there was none on the *Mayflower,* although its passengers had recently come from Holland where telescopes were invented a few years before.

The earliest mention in New England of the spy-glass, that has come to our attention, is an advertisement in the Oct. 14/21, 1734 issue of the *Boston Gazette* where Capt. Edward Ellis of Cold Lane, Boston, offered twenty shilling's reward, "and no questions ask'd", for the return of his "Prospective Glass, the Brass cap at the small end wanting." He had left it in the ferryboat between Boston and Charlestown a few nights before. After this date, from time to time, advertisements appear in the Boston newspapers mentioning prospective glasses and telescopes. "Mahogany Tellescopes" are offered for sale in October, 1751.

In 1758, Capt. Robert Rogers, in command of a scouting expedition sent out from Fort Edward during the French and Indian war, reported that at one point he "sent out Parties by Land, to look down the Lake with Prospective Glasses, which I had for that Purpose."—*Boston Gazette,* Apr. 3, 1758.

In the Marine Room Collection of the Peabody Museum at Salem, is a spy-glass four feet long, octagonal in form, two and one-half inches in diameter, with a short focusing tube. It was taken from a British prize vessel off the coast of Ireland, in 1779, by Capt. James Barr in his Salem privateer. Another glass of similar form, but longer and with a mahogany case, was used on a United States naval vessel about 1815. The spy-glass, familiar to everyone, in two or three sections, was used at sea through the first half of the nineteenth century and is often seen tucked under the left arm, in the portraits of ship-masters brought home from foreign ports. Many of these were excellent instruments, especially those from Dollond of London. There is also in the Salem collection a rude telescope or spy-glass five and one-half feet long with a copper case about three inches in diameter looking precisely like a section from a house water-conductor. It focuses by a small upper sliding section, fitted like a section of a stove funnel. This glass was brought from Nagasaki, Japan, by a Salem shipmaster about 1865. It had been used there to observe vessels coming into the harbor. It may be Dutch and it is evidently very old. Old spy-glasses were evidently very long for Joshua Kelly, in his "Compleat Modern Navigation Tutor," 1720, speaks of the "impractibility of managing a telescope twelve or fourteen feet long in the tossing, rolling motion of a ship at sea" in an attempt to observe Jupiter's satellites to obtain longitude.

The speed of a vessel was first obtained by throwing overboard a floating object at the bow and noting the time elapsed when it passed an observer at the stern. From this the log-line with "knots" was derived, with the fourteen and twenty-eight seconds sand glasses to record speed.

LOG-LINE

A "knot" indicates a geographical or sea mile which has been standardized at 6080 feet; the land or statute mile is 5280 feet, therefore, if a vessel is said to be sailing at the rate of thirteen knots, a railroad train going at the same speed would be running at the rate of fifteen miles an hour. The term "knot" is used solely to indicate rate of speed; the distance covered is always stated in nautical or sea miles. "Heaving the log" meant throwing out from the stern of a vessel a small float attached to a line running from a reel held clear of the rail, the float remaining stationary in the water. At the instant the log is "heaved" a sand glass is turned. On the line are knots (hence the term), pieces of marline or rags tied through the strands and spaced the same fraction of a mile apart,—about forty-six feet and six inches,—which twenty-eight seconds is the fraction of an hour,—about one one-hundred and twenty-eighth. Therefore, using a twenty-eight seconds glass and checking the line the instant the sand runs out, the knots and fractions paid out on the line will at once indicate the number of sea miles per hour which the vessel is going. This, of course, is doubled if the fourteen-seconds glass is used, which is done when the vessel is going very fast.

The old log and line has been superseded by various kinds of "patent logs" with revolving blades, first devised by Humfray Cole in 1578 and improved by others from time to time but, strange to say, not coming into general use for nearly three centuries. In the latest forms the rotating blades record the rate of progress by an indicator on the vessel which may be read at any time. The earliest reference so far found to the use of a device of this sort among our New England navigators is the "Gould's patent log" used by Captain George Crowninshield on his famous yacht *Cleopatra's Barge,* during the voyage to the Mediterranean in 1817. In September of the same year, Thomas Biggs, 66 South Front St., Philadelphia, advertised for sale patent logs and chronometers.

The record of the rate of speed of the vessel as indicated by the log, "heaved" at certain times in each "watch," was immediately entered on the slate or "log-board" and copied daily into a book kept for the purpose. This book naturally became the "log-book," which amplified with entries of other sorts relating to winds, weather, currents, shoals and experiences of the voyage, and often illustrated with sketches of coast lines, headlands and other vessels met, has become of great assistance to writers compiling marine history and scientific works relating to navigation.

The log-book day at sea corresponded to the astronomical day and extended from noon to noon in distinction from and overlapping the civil day which extended from midnight to midnight ; so that the log-book record for Monday, July 4, would begin Sunday noon, July 3, and extend to Monday noon, July 4, civil time, when the record for Tuesday, July 5, would begin. On shore, however, records were entered conforming to the shore or civil day usage.*

On the other hand, later usage, as shown by recent United States Government publications on navigation, is to begin the log-book day, when at sea, by dating it at noon of the civil day, numbering the hours to twenty-four and ending the day at noon of the suceeding day. Thus, Monday, July 4, log-book day, would begin on Monday, July 4, civil day, at noon and end at noon on Tuesday, July 5; the first twelve hours corresponding to those of the civil day, but, in the log-book, July 4, fourteen hours would be 2 A. M. July 5, civil day.†

Sounding for the depth of water has, of course, been practised ever since vessels were built and the lead and line was part of the outfit of every New England ship. The hand-lead for small vessels weighed about six pounds and had a line of twenty fathoms.

SOUNDING The deep-sea lead weighed up to eighty pounds,
LEADS was carried by men-of-war and large vessels, and
was provided with a much longer line. Roger Derby's *Province Galley* carried both forms in 1702. The lines are marked off in fathoms (6 feet) with bits of leather and colored rags, that various depths may be readily distinguished. In the base of the lead is a hollow space filled with tallow which, when it strikes, picks up sand, gravel and small stones, and thus indicates the character of the bottom, an important feature in following charts and sailing directions into harbors and over shoals.

*See Bowditch, "American Practical Navigator," edition 1817, page 204.
†See "American Practical Navigator," Washington, D. C., 1917, page 103.

Much skill is required in heaving the lead which by a swinging
motion is thrown forward to conform to the progress of the vessel so
that the line may be plumb with the observer and the lead strike
bottom as he takes the depth. The sounding lead was used by the
Romans before the Christian era and later in Britain by the Anglo
Saxons. It has to some extent been superseded by modern devices.

Charts were made in very ancient times but they were crude and
almost useless. The first nautical maps appeared in Italy at the end
of the thirteenth century and it is said that Bartholomew Columbus
brought the first one to England in 1489. The close of the sixteenth
century saw many mapmakers at work, including Gerard Mercator
whose name is perpetuated in the familiar scale charts in our geog-
raphies known as "Mercator's projection" which
CHARTS   were the sea charts in general use. Globes were
carried on ships in preference to charts in the
early days and what is known as "great circle" sailing was evolved
from them. Davis describes it in 1594 and it is possible that Cabot
knew of the theory a century before. Such a simple instrument as a
parallel ruler was not invented until late in the sixteenth century
and tables of logarithms and Gunter's scale by which navigators make
all their calculations were not known until 1620.

During the first century following the settlement of New England
it is probable that the small coasting and fishing vessels were navigated by dead reckoning and not venturing far beyond the sight of land
a compass was the only instrument carried. But the larger vessels
sailing from Boston, Salem, Portsmouth, Newport and other ports on
voyages to the West Indies, England and Spain, it would seem should
have carried instruments with which observations could be made to
obtain their approximate position. A search in the early probate
records of Essex County coast towns between 1634 and 1680 discloses
but thirteen references to nautical instruments in inventories and
wills. Sometimes they are listed as "marriners instruments" and in
one case a quadrant is valued at £1. Robert Gray of Salem, who died in
1661, possessed a "quadrant, a fore-staffe (cross-staff), a gunter's scale,
and a pair of Compasses." John Bradstreet, who died at Marblehead
the previous year owned "3 small sea books" valued at £1. 6s. The
inventory of the estate of Jonathan Browne of Salem, who died in
1667, discloses a "fore-staff," and that of the estate of John Silsby of
Salem, taken in 1676, lists "marriners instruments and callender, 14s."

Governor Winthrop records in his *Journal*, in 1637, that "Twenty men went in a pinnace to kill sea horse* at the Isle of Sable; and after six weeks returned home, and could not find the Island; but after another month, they set forth again with more skilful seamen, with intent to stay there all winter."

In a very detailed inventory made in Salem before a notary publick on Nov. 4, 1702, of the equipment of the ship *Province Galley,* 90 tons, owned by Roger Derby, the only instruments for navigation that appear are "Two Compasses, two ha[lf] ho[ur] glasses, a ha[lf] Watchglass, a ha[lf] minute glass . . . a hand lead line, a deep sea lead line."

The *Boston News-Letter,* of July 16, 1716, has the following advertisement:—"A Parcel of Mathematical Instruments, viz: Quadrants, Meridian Compasses, all sorts of Rules, black lead Pencils, and brass Ring Dials, etc. To be sold by Publick Vendue at the Crown Coffee House in King's Street, Boston, on Thursday next." The same issue has the advertisement of "William Walker in Merchants Row, near the Swing Bridge," who had quadrants for sale.

In looking back and noting the slow process of perfecting all nautical instruments, the wonder is how the old ships were navigated through distant seas without greater loss of life and vessels. These dangers may be realized by reference to old newspapers and letters, and to such records as the "Diary of Rev. William Bentley" of Salem, where nearly every Sunday some of his parishioners asked for prayers for friends at sea or for the loss of husband, son or brother. The shipmasters of Portsmouth, Salem, Boston, Newport and Providence, undertaking distant voyages, had few good charts—none for the new regions they visited—they had no chronometers; few had sextants, and their sextants and their compasses were frequently unreliable. And yet these men—most of them were scarcely past their majority in years—with the courage and enthusiasm of youth, in ships filled with valuable cargoes, entrusted to their care by wealthy owners, sailed into uncharted seas, visited unknown lands, and, all the while rarely reported, finally came safely back, to their everlasting credit and the enrichment of the country.

Capt. Benjamin Wright, a factor representing a Newport, R. I. merchant, wrote to his owner in 1771, from the Island of "Salamarr,"†

---

*The walrus which makes a noise somewhat resembling the neigh of a horse. It is valuable for its ivory and blubber.

†Savannah la Marr, Jamaica, W. I.

that he had "mett with trouble on account the officers of the *Diana,* differing and the mate leaving the Brigg, and has carried away his Servant, and two more of his Sailors has taken their departure, likewise Dan'l Watts Esq., by Profession a louzy Carpenter, has enloped before your long Boat was near finished. . . . I can but express my surprize that you and Capt. Buckly should ship a second mate which doth not understand Navigation."

We do not know exactly what instruments the old shipmasters carried with them on these voyages, but we do know that they were comparatively few and very inferior to those in use today. An idea of the paucity in some instances may be obtained from the story of the ship *Hannah,* condemned at Christiansand in 1810, in the protest of American shipmasters which is now preserved in the New Haven Historical Society collections. It reads: "We, the undersigned masters of American vessels now in the port of Christiansand, having heard with astonishment that one of the principal charges against the American brig *Hannah,* from Boston, bound direct to Riga, and condemned at the prize court at this place, is as follows,—that the said court have pronounced it absolutely impossible to cross the Atlantic without a chart or sextant. We therefore feel fully authorized to assert that we have frequently made voyages from America without the above articles, and we are fully persuaded that every seaman with common nautical knowledge can do the same."

We do not possess accurate knowledge of the instruments carried by Colonial shipmasters on their voyages to the West Indies or along our coast and across the Atlantic, but we do know that the early nineteenth century shipmasters were close observers. In his classical works on navigation, Maury pays them high compliment for the valuable assistance rendered to him in furnishing notes and observations on currents, shoals, coast-lines, compass variations and winds, for the charts and sailing directions which he compiled.

As this volume is largely devoted to pictures of vessels painted by artist living in home ports as well as abroad, any information relating to these men should be of interest. Unfortunately, SHIP PICTURES but little is known concerning many of them and this is particularly true of the water-colorists working in the principal Mediterranean ports where some of the finest pictures were painted. Pictures of New England vessels painted before the Revolution are almost unknown. The ship *Bethell* of Boston

(*See* Fig. 24), painted in 1748, is the oldest known painting of a ship and also one of the finest.. The three water-colors of the schooner *Baltick* of Salem (*See* Fig. 20), made in 1765 and now preserved by the Peabody Museum, Salem, are the oldest existing pictures of a Salem vessel.

About the year 1800 a considerable demand for ship pictures seems to have developed among the sea captains and merchants and there grew up a school of artists that specialized in water-colors of merchant vessels. Previous to 1830 nearly all of this work was done in water-colors but after that date painting in oils came into favor, especially in America and in the paintings done by Chinese artists. Some of this work was done by men living in the larger New England ports, self-taught and sometimes sailing in the vessels pictured. It usually was a labor of labor of love and though flat and frequently lifeless, it is certain that the lines were correct and that the rig was worked out with minutest care. Sign-painters also tried their hands in an effort to supply the demand, oftentimes with satisfying results. George Ropes of Salem, a sign-painter, deaf and dumb from birth, painted excellent pictures of the *America, Sukey, Fame, Glide, Two Brothers* and others and even elaborated his field to the extent of producing several pictures of naval battles and wharf scenes. By far the best work, however, was done at Marseilles, Genoa, Leghorn, Trieste, Smyrna and other Mediterranean ports. The Roux family at Marseilles, Anton, father and son, and Frederic and Francois, made numerous water-colors of vessels, all beautifully drawn and colored, and now highly esteemed. Painters of ship pictures were also working at Antwerp, Hamburg and Copenhagen and at a somewhat later date many ship pictures were brought home from China, done with great fidelity of detail by Chinese artists at Hong Kong, Lintin or Wampoa, and nearly always uniformly framed in hand-carved frames, painted black, of so similar a pattern that they are easily recognized. Sometimes the officer who kept the log-book illustrated his log with sketches, occasionally in colors, of his ship or other vessels met on the voyage. But unless a vessel visited one of these foreign ports where painters of ship pictures worked or its picture was painted by some local artist, it never was made. Of all the sea-going New England vessels probably not one in ten was ever pictured. Some of the later ships, after 1860, were photographed as nearly every ship of note is today.

Many of the vessels pictured in this volume are connected with tales of adventure or disaster. The ship *Ulysses* (*See* Fig. 293) is shown with a temporary rudder, adjusted sea at during a gale by a device that brought a gold medal from the American Philosophical Society and commendation to her master, Capt. William Mugford. The brig *Eunice* (*See* Fig. 88) may be seen surrounded by a barrel made of planking, being rolled into the water at St. Paul's Island in the Indian Ocean, after undergoing repairs necessary to enable her master to return safely to the wharf at Salem. The ship *Volusia* (*See* Fig. 298) is just striking the beach at Cape Cod, in February, 1802, in a disastrous wreck in which most of the crew lost their lives. The *Mount Vernon* is seen escaping from a French fleet near Gibraltar in 1799 (*See* Fig. 199) and the ship *Belisarius* is just leaving Crownin-shield's wharf on which are standing the owners and relatives of the ship's company (*See* Fig. 22). There is a harrowing tale of disaster at sea and suffering and death connected with the ship *Margaret* which sailed from Naples in 1810 on her last voyage (*See* Fig. 180). This vessel was in Japan in 1801 when that country was closed to all foreign trade save a vessel sent annually from Batavia by the Dutch East India Company. A water-color of the ship *Hercules,* of much pictorial interest (*See* Fig. 132), recalls the fact that Lucien Bonaparte and his family sailed from Naples on this vessel, in 1819, bound for the United States, but through misadventure were intercepted by the British cruiser *Pomona* and taken into Malta. The *Hercules* finally became a whaler and was lost in the Pacific in 1847 after forty-two years of successful voyaging.

It has not been possible, because of limited space, to attempt to include in this volume the life-histories of the vessels here pictured. Such information is widely scattered and awaits the industry of the patient student. Moreover, many volumes would be required to relate the story of the adventurous careers and commercial successes of the white-winged messengers that carried the tale of New England's sea-borne commerce to nearly every port in the known world.

PAINTERS OF SHIP PICTURES

AYLWARD, W. J. (1875—), born in Milwaukee and worked in New York; in 1904.*

BARTOLL, SAMUEL, Marblehead and Salem. House painter and sign-painter; married in 1785; was working in Salem as late as 1825; painted mural decorations, fire-boards, military flags, etc.

BATEMAN, CHARLES E., Newburyport; made pencil drawings in 1853.

BROWN, HARRY, Portland, Maine; in 1870.

CAMMILLIERI, NICOLAI (sometimes signed Nicolay Carmillieri), Marseilles; in 1806-1807.

CARLOTTA, A., Port Mahon, Minorca, Spain; in 1822.

CARMILETTI, E., Smyrna; in 1831.

CLEVELAND, WILLIAM (1777-1845), Salem.

CORNE, MICHELE FELICE (1757-1845), Naples, Salem, and Newport. Came to Salem from Naples in the ship *Mount Vernon* in 1799; painted many pictures of ships and during the War of 1812 a series of naval battles which were exhibited in Salem and Boston and from which he gained a competency and removed to Newport, R. I. where he lived until his death. (*See* Mason's Reminiscences of Newport, p. 330) Many of Corne's paintings of naval engagements were engraved for the popular naval histories of the War of 1812—"The Naval Monument, Naval Temple, and Naval Battles."

CORSINI, RAFFAELE, Smyrna; in 1849-1852.

DANNENBERG, F.; in 1805.

DREW, CLEMENT (1807-1889), born in Kingston, Mass.; worked in Boston; was living in Maine in 1889; in 1844-1851.

EATON, WILLIAM BRADLEY (1836-1896), Salem, in 1884.

ERUZIONE, ZI., Palermo (?), Italy; in 1822.

EVANS AND ARNOLD, New Orleans, La.; in 1850.

GAVAZZONE, DOMENICO, Genoa, Italy; in 1848.

*Dates thus entered indicate the period in which the artist worked or the year in which there is a known painting.

GORE, CHARLES, London, England. "English marine draughtsman, flourished about the end of the 18th century. There are several of his drawings in the Cracherode collection in the British Museum." Bryan's "Dictionary of Painters and Engravers," London 1903; in 1787.

HOWARD, JOSEPH, Salem; in 1799.

HUGE, I. F., Bridgeport, Conn.; in 1845.

JOHNSON, MARSHALL (1846 - 1921), Boston.

LUSCOMB, WILLIAM HENRY (1805 - 1866), Salem. He was born at Ballston, N. Y. The Salem directory gives his occupation as "a sign and fancy painter." He made many oil paintings of Salem vessels and his pencil sketches though small were excellent; unfortunately, however, few have been preserved. Was doing his best work between 1845 and 1855.

LUZ, JOHN, Venice, Italy; in 1850.

McFARLANE, D.; in 1861 - 1864.

MACPHERSON, MURDOCK (1841 - 1915), Salem. Born at Fort Simpson, Rupert Land, Canada; graduated at McGill College and studied law with Hon. A. C. Macdonald; came to Salem in 1873 and taught music and drawing. Between 1902 and 1914 made many remarkable copies of old water-colors of ships and similar work. (*See* Figs. 27, 165, 206, 226, 282).

MAZZINGHI, PETER, Leghorn, Italy; in 1831 - 1833.

MELBORO——, I. B., in 1830.

MONTARDIER, ——, Havre, France; in 1810.

MOOY, JAN.; in 1818.

MORSE F. A.; in 1885.

MORSE, GEORGE FREDERICK (1834—), Portland, Maine. Has made many admirable studies in oils, especially landscapes, with a few marines and pencil sketches of vessels in Portland harbor in 1858.

NORTON, CHARLES W., Detroit, Mich.; in 1875.

NORTON, WILLIAM EDWARD (1853 - 1916), Boston. Studied under William F. Hunt and George Inness.

PELLEGRINI, HRE, (sometimes signed Pellegrin) Marseilles; in 1831-1848.

PETERSEN, JACOB (1774 - 1854), Copenhagen; in 1817 - 1838.

PHIPPEN, JOHN, Salem; in 1790.

PITMAN, THOMAS, Marblehead; about 1850.

POCOCK, NICHOLAS (1741-1821), London, England. A shipmaster and afterwards a marine painter of considerable merit.

POLLI, FELICE, Trieste, Italy; in 1830.

RALEIGH, C. S.; about 1840.

RESSMAN, FRANCISCO, Trieste, Italy; in 1809.

ROPES, GEORGE (1788-1819), Salem. His father was lost at sea in 1807 leaving a widow and nine children. George Ropes, though deaf and dumb from birth, was the chief support of his widowed mother and brothers and sisters. While a pupil of Michele Felice Corne, in 1802, he began to paint pictures of vessels and continued to do so through life. He was a carriage and sign-painter by trade. (*See* Diary of Rev. William Bentley, Vol. IV, p. 573.)

ROUX, ANTON (1765-1835), Marseilles. He was a hydrographer established on one of the quays in Marseilles. "He greatly admired the Provencal artist Joseph Vernet whose works he copied. His ship paintings are noted for their accuracy of detail."

ROUX, ANTON, *fils aine* (1799-1872), Marseilles. Son of Anton Roux, who "continued the double profession of his father but his work as an artist was inferior."

ROUX, FREDERIC (1805-1882), Marseilles, Havre and Paris. Son of Anton Roux, "entered the studio of Horace Vernet, where he gained a flexibilty of vision and boldness of touch which were lacking in his brother Anton's work."

ROUX, FRANCOIS (1811-1882), Marseilles. Son of Anton Roux, "obtained the title of painter to the Ministry of Marine and distinguished himself in his genre pictures."

RUSSELL, BENJAMIN (1804-1885), New Bedford; in 1860. A well-known and highly esteemed painter of whaling vessels.

RUSSELL, EDWARD J. (1835-1906), Boston. Of English birth, lived in Boston and did excellent work as a copyist.

SALMON, ROBERT, Liverpool and Boston. Came to Boston in 1828 and painted industriously until his death, not only marine but other subjects. His views of Boston harbor and the shipping are highly prized. Left an annotated list of his paintings and sales covering the period of 1828-1840, copies of which are at the Boston Public Library and the Peabody Museum, Salem.

SMITH, W. H.; in 1868.

SOUTHWARD, GEORGE (1803 - 1876), Salem ; portrait painter and copyist. *See* Fig. 190.

SPICE, J., Amsterdam, Holland ; in 1856.

SPINN, J., Amsterdam, Holland ; in 1842.

STONE, EDMUND, Beverly. A sailor on the ship *George,* of Salem, of which he painted many pictures about 1820.

STUBBS, W. P., Boston. Painted many pictures of New England vessels in oils. Worked in Boston between 1876 and 1894.

SUNQUA, a Chinese artist at Lintin, China, who painted many ship pictures between 1835 and 1845, of which two signed examples are known.

T. P. ; in 1835.

TORREY, CHARLES (1869-1921), Brookline, Mass. Painted many excellent ship pictures in oil colors between 1915 and 1921, including copies.

TURNER, ROSS STERLING (1848-1915), Salem. Painted several excellent marines and also made copies of water-colors.

VITTALUGA, ANTOINE, Genoa, Italy ; in 1817-1829.

WALTER AND SON, 7 Pleasant St., Liverpool, England ; in 1830.

WALTERS, SAMUEL ; about 1870.

WARD, WILLIAM, Salem ; in 1799-1800.

WEST, BENJAMIN FRANKLIN (1818-1854), Salem. The Salem directory lists him as "Painter, 125 Essex St." He was self-taught, worked in oils and his work though somewhat stiff was accurate in its details.

WEYTZ, P., Antwerp, Belgium. His paintings were done mostly on glass ; in 1840-1844.

WHALL, CAPT. W. B., Boston.

WHITE, GEORGE MEWANJEE (1849-1915), Salem. Water-colorist and also did etchings.

WILSON, JAMES, Liverpool, England ; in 1860.

YORK, WILLIAM ; in 1879.

ADDITIONS AND CORRECTIONS

Fig. 6. Painted in 1799 by M. F. Corne.

Fig. 10. 211 tons. Starbuck says, lost in 1851, in his "History of the American Whale Fishery."

Fig. 12. Painted at Copenhagen; Kronberg Castle, Elsinore, in the background.

Fig. 17. *Ship* "Austerlitz," 415 tons, built at Medford in 1833. Abandoned at sea Nov. 19, 1851.

Fig. 27. Topsail schooner.

Fig. 29. 319 tons, built at Medford in 1816.

Fig. 31. Ship "Canton Packet," 274 tons, built at Swanzey, Mass., in 1836. Re-rigged as a bark. Stranded Sept. 12, 1839, near Hernberg, C. T.

Fig. 35. From an oil painting by *D.* McFarlane.

Fig. 36. From a lithograph after a drawing by E. N. Russell.

Fig. 37. Painted in 1844.

Fig. 57. Hermaphrodite brig.

Fig. 58. *Brig* "Cygnet."

Fig. 60. 218 tons, built at Newbury in 1829. Wrecked at Chatham, Mass., in 1854. Painted at Copenhagen.

Fig. 68. Topsail schooner in picture. Registered as a brig.

Fig. 70. The quick passage of this vessel is now very generally questioned.

Fig. 83. Painted by Robert Salmon.

Fig. 86. Painted by Montardier at Havre.

Fig. 88. The original of this picture is dated 1806.

Fig. 92. Double-topsail schooner. The gaff-topsail is very unusual.

Fig. 94. Original painting is not at the Peabody Museum, Salem.

Fig. 101. 179 tons, built at Hanover, Mass., in 1792. Painted at Nagasaki in 1799, by a Dutch artist.

Fig. 110. 273 tons.

Fig. 113. Painted by William P. Stubbs.

Fig. 117. Painted by "Smith, 1857."

Fig. 121. This representation of the "Grand Turk," is a copy of an engraving of the ship "Hall," in Hutchinson's "Naval Architecture," London, 1777.

(65)

Fig. 132. Painted at Naples in 1809.

Fig. 139. Painted by Benjamin F. West.

Fig. 148. Painted by Clement Drew.

Fig. 154. Painted by Benjamin F. West. The other half of this painting is Fig. 246.

Fig. 155. *Brig* "Juliana."

Fig. 156. Bark *"Juniata,"* painted by *Corsini*.

Fig. 157. Painted in 1902 by E. N. Russell.

Fig. 159. Painted by Benjamin Russell.

Fig. 166. Topsail schooner.

Fig. 172. Hermaphrodite brig. Painted by a Chinese artist, showing the light-ship off Shanghai.

Fig. 174. Clipper-ship "Lucy S. *Wills.*"

Fig. 175. 163 tons, built at Plymouth in 1805.

Fig. 192. Reproduction of a photograph by Stebbins of the ship "Panay," 1190 tons, built at Boston in 1877, wrecked on the Island of Simara, P. I., July 12, 1890.

Fig. 194. Reproduced from the *original* painting.

Fig. 195. From a lithograph by D. H. Crosby of Boston.

Fig. 203. Painted on glass by P. Weytz about 1840, at Antwerp.

Fig. 205. Painted by Benjamin F. West. The Salem fire occurred in June, *1914*.

Fig. 227. The drawing shows a double-topsail schooner, but she was carried on the Government records as a brig. *See also* Fig. 92.

Fig. 232. Painted by Hre Pellegrin at Marseilles in 1844.

Fig. 234. Built in *1799*.

Fig. 238. Double-topsail schooner, commanded in *1796*.

Fig. 246. Painted by Benjamin F. West. Same vessel as Fig. 243. The other half of this painting in Fig. 154.

Fig. 248. Probably painted at Leghorn.

Fig. 250. Shows the vessel coming out of Leghorn. The obscure signature resembles. "A. Prit—."

NOTE. Snow rig—a close examination of original paintings discloses the fact that the following so-called "brigs", carried the subsidiary mast of the "snow" (*see* page 30), viz:—Figs. 30, 38, 58, 80, 82, 118, 127, 133, 162, 175, 176, 178, 181, 200, 201, 204, 206, 214, 215, 216, 223, 225, 226, 240, 248, 250.

THE SAILING SHIPS OF NEW ENGLAND

1748—1907

[2] BARK "ABBY BACON," 473 TONS, BUILT AT GOSPORT, VA., IN 1861,
COMMANDED BY CAPT. JOSEPH W. BESSOM OF MARBLEHEAD.

[3] BARK "ALBERS," 360 TONS, BUILT AT TOPSHAM, ME. IN 1844.

[4] SHIP "ALBUS," COMMANDED BY CAPT. MICHAEL B.
GREGORY OF MARBLEHEAD.

[5] BRIGANTINE "ALERT," OF NEWBURYPORT, 139 TONS, BUILT
AT AMESBURY IN 1806, CAPT. S. HERRICK, MASTER, ENTERING
MARSEILLES, DEC. 13, 1806.

[6] SHIP "AMERICA," 3d, OF SALEM, 654 TONS, BUILT IN FRANCE.

[7] SHIP "ANN AND HOPE," 550 TONS, BUILT IN 1798 BY BENJAMIN
TALLMAN FOR BROWN AND IVES OF PROVIDENCE, R. I.

[8] SHIP "AMERICA" (4th), 437 TONS, BUILT IN 1804,
COMMANDED BY CAPT. BENJAMIN CROWNINSHIELD, JR.

This ship was cut down and altered to 331 tons in 1812 and became the famous privateer "America." From a water-color by Anton Roux, showing the ship at anchor at Marseilles in 1806.

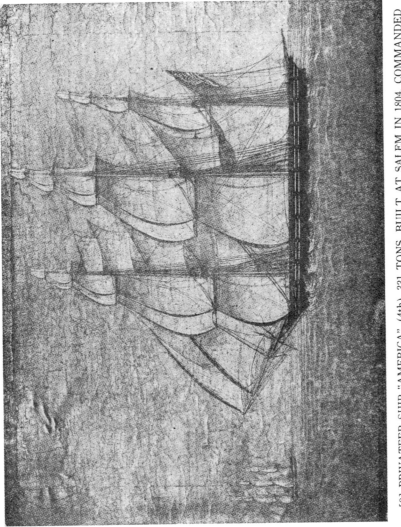

[9] PRIVATEER SHIP "AMERICA" (4th), 331 TONS, BUILT AT SALEM IN 1804, COMMANDED BY CAPT. JAMES CHEVER.

From an oil painting by George Ropes of Salem, painted in 1815, showing the chase of H. B. M. Packet "Princess Elizabeth," on Feb. 27, 1815.

[10] WHALING SHIP "ANN ALEXANDER," OF NEW BEDFORD.
Attacked by a whale in 1850 and sunk in a few minutes.

[11] SHIP "ANN MARIA," 489 TONS, BUILT AT ESSEX, MASS.,
IN 1843, DAVID PINGREE AND CHARLES MILLETT, OWNERS.

[12] SHIP "ARBELLA," OF SALEM, 404 TONS, BUILT AT BATH,
MAINE, IN 1825.

[13] BRIG "ANTELOPE" OF BOSTON, 370 TONS, BUILT IN 1843 AT EAST BOSTON, FOR RUSSELL & CO.

Used in the opium trade between India and Canton.

[14] SHIP "ARCHER," 1095 TONS, BUILT AT SOMERSET IN 1853.
From a painting by a Chinese artist made in Hong Kong.

[15] SHIP "AURORA" OF SALEM, 1396 TONS, BUILT AT CHELSEA IN 1853

[16]. SHIP "ARGONAUT," 570 TONS, BUILT AT MEDFORD IN 1849. OWNED BY JOHN ELLERTON LODGE OF BOSTON.

[17] "AUSTERLITZ," CAPT. WILLIAM HAMMOND OF MARBLE-
HEAD, MASTER, ENTERING THE PORT OF HAVRE, JANUARY 9, 1834.

[18] SHIP "AUSTRALIA," OF SALEM, 534 TONS, BUILT AT
MEDFORD IN 1849.

Sold to Boston owners in 1861 and afterwards wrecked about 1868 at Maulmain.
From a painting at the Peabody Museum, Salem, showing the ship
"entering the new harbor of Marseilles, June, 1857."

[19] BARK "AZOF," 297 TONS, BUILT AT MEDFORD IN 1844.

[20] TOPSAIL SCHOONER "BALTICK," OF SALEM, COMING OUT OF
ST. EUSTATIA, NOV. 16, 1765.
The earliest picture of a Salem vessel.

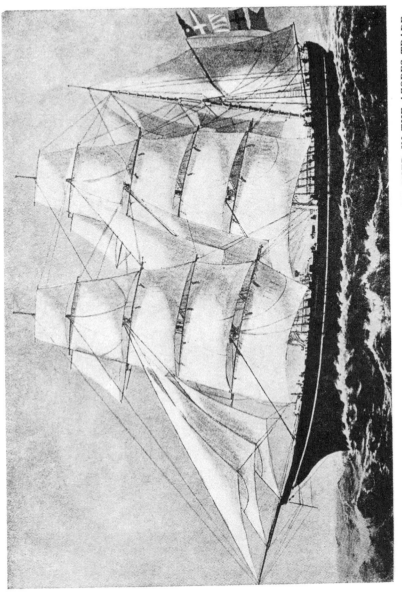

[21] BARK "AZOR," 431 TONS, BUILT AT EAST BOSTON IN 1853, AND USED IN THE AZORES TRADE.

[22] SHIP "BELISARIUS," 209 TONS, BUILT AT SALEM IN 1794.
Lost near Tunis in April, 1810.   From a water-color by M. F. Corne,
showing the vessel leaving a wharf in Salem.

[23] SHIP "BONETTA," OF SALEM, 227 TONS, BUILT AT
DUXBURY IN 1800.
From a water-color painted at Leghorn in 1805.

[24] SHIP BETHELL," OF BOSTON, CAPT. ISAAC FREEMAN, MASTER, OWNED BY
JOSIAH QUINCY AND EDWARD JACKSON.

From an oil painting made about 1748, showing the vessel in two positions, now owned by the Massachusetts
Historical Society. The earliest painting known of a New England ship.

[25] SHIP "BORNEO," 297 TONS, BUILT AT SALEM IN 1831.
Afterwards altered to a bark and abandoned in the North Atlantic, Jan. 1, 1854.
From a water-color painted in Genoa.

[26] SHIP "BOSTONIAN," 1099 TONS, BUILT AT EAST
BOSTON, IN 1854 BY DONALD McKAY.

[27] SCHOONER "BRENDA" OF BOSTON, BUILT IN 1852, AT
PORTSMOUTH, N. H.
Used by Russell & Co., in the opium trade between India and Canton.

[28] SHIP "BROOKLINE" OF SALEM, 349 TONS, BUILT AT MEDFORD,
IN 1831. LATER BECAME A WHALER OUT OF NEW LONDON, CONN.
From a painting showing the ship leaving Salem for Manila, July 26, 1839.

[29] SHIP "CADMUS," CAPT. SAMUEL IVES, MASTER.
From a water-color by Anton Roux, painted at Marseilles in 1822.

[30] BRIG "CAMBRIAN," 196 TONS, BUILT AT SALEM IN 1818.
From a water-color by Frederic Roux, painted in 1826.

[31] BARK "CANTON PACKET," OF BOSTON, OWNED BY
J. & T. H. PERKINS.

[32] SHIP "CARNATIC," 602 TONS, BUILT AT SACO, ME., IN 1847,
ENTERING THE HARBOR OF LIVERPOOL.

[33] SHIP "CAROLINA," OF SALEM, 395 TONS, BUILT AT MEDFORD IN 1836.

[34] SHIP "CARRINGTON," 598 TONS, BUILT AT WARREN, R. I. IN 1847.

[35] SHIP "CASTILLIAN," 993 TONS, BUILT AT NEWBURYPORT IN 1849, BY JOHN CURRIER, JR.
From an oil painting by Macfarlane, showing the ship off Liverpool in 1861.

[36] WHALING BARK "CATALPA" OF NEW BEDFORD, 261 TONS, BUILT AT MEDFORD IN 1844.
From a painting showing the rescue of Fenian prisoners at Australia, in 1876.

[37] SHIP "CARTHAGE," 426 TONS, BUILT AT SALEM IN 1837.
From an oil painting by Clement Drew of Boston.

[38] BRIG "CENTURION," OF SALEM, 205 TONS, BUILT AT HAVERHILL IN 1822.
From a water-color painted about 1825.

[39] BARK "CERES," OF SALEM, 387 TONS, BUILT AT MEDFORD IN 1846.

[40] BARK "CHALCEDONY," 214 TONS, BUILT AT MEDFORD IN 1825.
From a painting by Benjamin F. West.

[41] SHIP "CHALLENGE," 2006 TONS, BUILT AT NEW YORK
IN 1851 BY W. H. WEBB.

[42] SHIP "CHARIOT OF FAME," 1573 TONS, BUILT BY DONALD MCKAY IN 1853.

[43] SHIP "CHARLEMAGNE," BUILT IN 1824.
From a water-color by Frederic Roux, painted at Paris in 1828.

[44] SHIP "CHARLOTTE," OF BOSTON, 390 TONS, BUILT AT
PORTSMOUTH, N. H., IN 1832.

[45] SHIP "CHINA," 370 TONS, BUILT AT SALEM IN 1817.
After a water-color signed "Gueissippi ———."

[46] SHIP "CLAUDIUS," BUILT AT MEDFORD IN 1836
BY P. & J. O. CURTIS.

[47] HERMAPHRODITE BRIG "CLEOPATRA'S BARGE," 191 TONS, BUILT AT SALEM IN 1816. A pleasure-yacht built for George Crowninshield. From a water-color painted at Genoa by Antoine Vittaluga, now at the Peabody Museum, Salem. The stripe on the port side of this vessel was painted in herring-bone pattern; on the starboard side it was plain.

[48] HERMAPHRODITE BRIG "CLEOPATRA'S BARGE," 191 TONS, BUILT AT SALEM IN 1816.
A pleasure-yacht built for George-Crowninshield. From a water-color painted at Genoa, by
Antoine Vittaluga, showing the vessel entering the harbor.

[49] SHIP "COLUMBIA," OF BOSTON, BUILT AT SCITUATE.
The first Boston vessel to visit the northwest coast and to circumnavigate the
globe.   From a drawing at the Bostonian Society showing an attack
by natives in the Straits of Juan de Fuca.

[50] SHIP "COLUMBUS," OF BOSTON, COMMANDED IN 1824 BY
CAPT. SAMUEL TUCKER OF MARBLEHEAD.
From a painting by Jacob Peterson showing the ship passing Crownburg
Castle on the voyage from Copenhagen.

[51] SHIP "COLUMBIANA," OF BOSTON, 630 TONS, BUILT AT MEDFORD IN 1837.
Abandoned at sea in 1854.

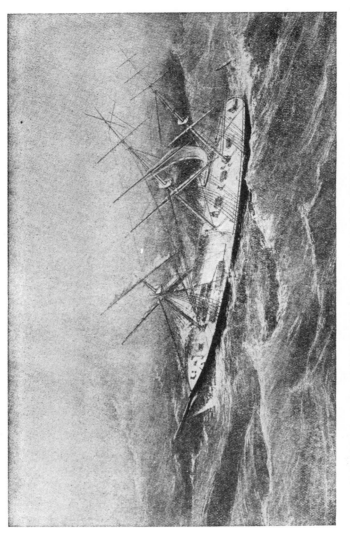

[52] CLIPPER-SHIP "COMET," IN A HURRICANE OFF BERMUDA, OCTOBER, 1852.

[53] CLIPPER-SHIP "COMET," OWNED BY GEN. EDWARD CARRINGTON
OF PROVIDENCE, R. I.

[54] SHIP "CORDELIA," OF BOSTON, HOMEWARD BOUND FROM
LEGHORN ABOUT 1830.

[55] UNITED STATES FRIGATE "CONSTITUTION," 2200 TONS, BUILT AT BOSTON IN 1797.

[56] BRIG "CRUGER," 154 TONS, BUILT IN MARYLAND IN 1788.
OWNED BY ELIAS HASKET DERBY OF SALEM.

[57] BRIG "CURLEW," COMMANDED BY CAPT. JOSEPH GREGORY,
BUILT IN MARBLEHEAD AND SOLD IN BATAVIA IN 1857.

[58] SHIP "CYGNET," 215 TONS, BUILT AT SALEM IN 1822.
From a water-color by "Anthony Roux, the Son, at Marseilles, 1824."

[59] BARK "CYNTHIA," 374 TONS, BUILT AT HAVERHILL IN 1833.
From a painting by Sunqua, a Chinese artist at Lintin in 1838.

[60] BRIG "CZARINA," OF BOSTON.
From a painting made in 1838 by J. Petersen.

[61] SHIP "DANIEL I. TENNEY," 1687 TONS, BUILT
AT NEWBURYPORT IN 1875.
A very deep ship, having three full decks. From a painting showing
the ship passing Pier Head, Havre, France, outward bound.

[62] SHIP "DANIEL WEBSTER," 1187 TONS, BUILT AT EAST
BOSTON IN 1850 BY DONALD McKAY.
From a painting showing the ship rescuing the passengers of the
immigrant ship "Unicorn," on November 9, 1851.

[63] SHIP "DANUBE," 908 TONS, BUILT AT BATH, ME., IN 1854.

[64] SHIP "DANUBE," 908 TONS, BUILT AT BATH, ME., IN 1854.
From an oil painting showing the ship at anchor off Victoria, Hong Kong.

[65] SHIP "DASHING WAVE," 1239 TONS, BUILT AT PORTSMOUTH,
N. H., IN 1853.
From a pencil drawing made in 1855.

[66] SHIP "DASHING WAVE," 1239 TONS, BUILT AT PORTSMOUTH,
N. H., IN 1853.
From a painting showing the ship entering Boston harbor in 1855.

[67] SHIP "DERBY," 1062 TONS, BUILT AT CHELSEA IN 1855.
From a painting by a Chinese artist showing the ship "entering Hong Kong,
March 13, 1864."

[68] HERMAPHRODITE BRIG "DIOMEDE," 223 TONS, BUILT AT
SALEM IN 1809, JOHN CROWINSHIELD, OWNER.

[69] FOUR-MASTED BARKENTINE "DORIS," 944 TONS, BUILT AT
BELFAST, MAINE, IN 1894.

[70] SHIP "DREADNAUGHT," 1414 TONS, BUILT AT NEWBURYPORT IN 1853.
Made the passage from Sandy Hook to Queenstown in 9 days and 17 hours. Wrecked in 1869 on
Cape Penas, near Terre del Fuego.

[71] BARK "DRAGON," 289 TONS, BUILT AT NEWBURY IN 1850.
From an oil painting probably by Benjamin F. West of Salem.

[72] SHIP "DROMO," 306 TONS, BUILT AT PLYMOUTH IN 1828.
From a water-color showing the ship off the port of Marseilles in 1836.

[73] SHIP "EDWARD HYMAN," 1056 TONS, BUILT AT
CASTINE, MAINE, IN 1855.

[74] BARK "EDWARD KOPPISCH," 249 TONS, BUILT AT NEWBURY IN 1845.
From a painting by Benjamin F. West about 1854.

[75] BARK "ELIZA," 240 TONS, BUILT AT SALEM IN 1823.
Sailed for California, with passengers, in December, 1848. From a painting
by Benjamin F. West.

[76] BRIG "ELIZA," OWNED BY BROWN & IVES OF PROVIDENCE, R. I.
From a water-color showing the brig leaving Leghorn in 1805.

[77] SHIP "ELIZA," 272 TONS, BUILT AT SALEM IN 1817.
From a water-color painted at Leghorn in 1829.

[78] WHALING SHIP "ELIZA ADAMS," 403 TONS, BUILT AT
FAIRHAVEN, MASS., IN 1835.
From a painting by C. S. Raleigh, at the Peabody Museum, Salem.

[79] BRIG "ELIZA AND MARY," 132 TONS, BUILT AT BOSTON IN 1804.
From a painting made in 1822. Went ashore near Amboy, N. J. in 1823
and abandoned.

[80] BRIG "ELIZA ANN," 137 TONS, BUILT AT CHARLESTOWN IN 1828.
Lost at sea in 1837. From a water-color painted by Francois Roux
at Marseilles in 1836.

[81] SHIP "ELIZA ANN," OF SALEM, 370 TONS, BUILT AT BALTIMORE,
MARYLAND, IN 1835.
From a painting by a Chinese artist at Whampoa.

[82] BRIG "ELIZA BURGESS," OF SALEM, 176 TONS, BUILT AT COHASSET
IN 1838.
From a painting by William H. Luscomb.

[83] SHIP "EMERALD," 359 TONS, BUILT AT BOSTON IN 1822.

[84] SHIP "EMPORIUM," OF BOSTON, 309 TONS, BUILT AT WISCASSET,
MAINE, IN 1832.
From a water-color by Anton Roux, sen., painted at Marseilles in 1833.

[85] CLIPPER-SHIP "EMPRESS OF THE SEA," 1756 TONS, BUILT AT
EAST BOSTON BY DONALD McKAY IN 1853.
From a pencil drawing by Charles E. Bateman of Newburyport.

[86] SHIP "ERIN," OF SALEM, 270 TONS, BUILT AT NEW YORK IN 1810.

[87] UNITED STATES FRIGATE "ESSEX," 860 TONS, BUILT AT SALEM IN 1799.
The largest vessel built at Salem. From a water-color by Joseph Howard, at the
Peabody Museum, Salem.

[88] BRIG "EUNICE" OF SALEM, 145 TONS, BUILT AT BARNSTABLE IN 1803.
From a water-color by Anton Roux, showing device for launching the vessel after
cleaning its bottom at St. Paul Island in 1817.

[89] BRIGANTINE "EXPERIMENT," OF NEWBURYPORT, 114 TONS, BUILT
AT AMESBURY IN 1803.
From a water-color painted in 1807 by Nicolay Carmillieri.

[90] SHIP "FANNY," OF SALEM, 150 TONS, BUILT AT FREEPORT, ME., IN 1796.
From a water-color by M. Corne painted in 1801, now at the Peabody Museum, Salem.

[91] THE LAUNCH OF THE SHIP "FAME," 363 TONS, AT SALEM IN 1802.
From an oil painting by George Ropes of Salem, at the Essex Institute, Salem.

[92] TOPSAIL-SCHOONER "FAME," OF SALEM, 62 TONS, BUILT AT
IPSWICH IN 1795.
From a water-color painted in 1800 by William Ward.

[93] SHIP "FEARLESS," 1183 TONS, BUILT AT EAST BOSTON
IN 1853, AND OWNED BY W. F. WELD & CO.

[94] SHIP "FLORENCE," 1045 TONS, BUILT AT EAST BOSTON IN 1856 FOR J. M. AND
R. B. FORBES, FOR THE EAST INDIA TRADE.

The first American vessel to enter the port of Nagaski. From a painting at the
Peabody Museum, Salem.

[95] SHIP "FLYING EAGLE," 1094 TONS, BUILT AT
NEWCASTLE, MAINE, IN 1853.
After an oil painting made at Hong Kong by a Chinese artist.

[96] SHIP "FLYING FISH," OF BOSTON, 1350 TONS, BUILT
AT EAST BOSTON IN 1851 BY DONALD McKAY.
Built for the California trade.   Foundered in the China Sea.

[97] SHIP "FLYING CLOUD," OF BOSTON, 1782 TONS, BUILT AT EAST BOSTON IN 1851
BY DONALD McKAY.

One of the fastest clippers ever launched. One day sailed 433 1-2 statute miles. Finally sold to Liverpool, England, owners and at last destroyed by fire at St. John, N. B., in 1874.

[98] SHIP "FORMOSA," OF SALEM, 1252 TONS, BUILT AT EAST BOSTON IN 1868.
Used in the Australian trade. Wrecked January 3, 1880 on the Western Tweeling Island, Atlas Straits, near
Java. From a painting by a Chinese artist at Hong Kong.

[99] SHIP "FRANCIS," 297 TONS, BUILT AT SALEM IN 1807.
From a water-color by Anton Roux, 1816, at the Peabody Museum, Salem.

[100] SHIP "FRANK JOHNSON, 529 TONS, BUILT AT CAPE ELIZABETH,
MAINE, IN 1850.
From a water-color by Frederic Roux, painted at Havre in 1851.

[101] SHIP "FRANKLIN," OF BOSTON, AND HER CAPTAIN, JAMES DEVEREUX OF SALEM.
Traded with Japan in 1799, the third American vessel to do so.

[102] SHIP "FREDONIA," 406 TONS, BUILT AT NEWBURYPORT
IN 1827.
From a water-color showing the vessel off Havre in 1830.

[103] SHIP "FRIENDSHIP," 342 TONS, BUILT AT SALEM IN 1797.

[104] SHIP "GAME COCK," OF BOSTON, 1320 TONS, BUILT BY
SAMUEL HALL OF EAST BOSTON, IN 1850.
Condemned in 1880 at the Cape of Good Hope.

[105] SHIP "GAME COCK," 1320 TONS, BUILT AT EAST BOSTON IN 1850.

[106] SHIP "GANGES," 215 TONS, BUILT AT SCITUATE IN 1806.
From a water-color made a Marseilles showing the ship leaving for
India in 1819.

[107] SHIP "GEORGE," 328 TONS, BUILT AT SALEM IN 1814.
From a painting by Edmund Stone of Beverly.

[108] SHIP "GENEVA," 458 TONS, BUILT AT NEWBURY IN 1838.
From a painting showing the ship passing Elsinore Castle, Oct. 9, 1844.

[109] SNOW "GEORGE," FROM A DRAWING MADE ABOUT
1793 IN A LOG BOOK NOW AT THE MASSACHUSETTS
HISTORICAL SOCIETY.

[110] WHALING SHIP "GEORGE," OF NEW BEDFORD.
From a water-color painted at Havre by Montardier.

[111] SHIP "GEORGE WEST," 1071 TONS, BUILT AT NEWBURY
IN 1855.

[112] BARK "GERTRUDE," OF BOSTON, 507 TONS, BUILT AT
BATH, MAINE, IN 1852.

[113] BARK "GLIDE," 295 TONS, BUILT AT SALEM IN 1861.
Wrecked at Tamatave, Madagascar, in 1887.

[114] SHIP "GLIDE," 306 TONS, BUILT AT SALEM IN 1811.
From a water-color by "Anton Roux fils aine a Marseille, 1823."

[115] SHIP "GOLDEN FLEECE," OF BOSTON, 1535 TONS, BUILT AT EAST BOSTON IN 1855. OWNED BY W. F. WELD & CO. CONDEMNED AT MONTEVIDEO IN 1878.

[116] SHIP "GOLDEN EAGLE," BUILT AT MEDFORD IN 1852.
From a painting made at Hong Kong, China.

[117] SHIP "GOLDEN WEST," 1441 TONS, BUILT AT BOSTON
IN 1852. CAPT. S. H. CURWIN OF SALEM, MASTER.

The Letter of Marque Brig Grand Turk of 18 Guns W.ᵐ Austin Com.ᵈᵉʳ Saluting Marseilles. 1815

[118] BRIG "GOVERNOR ENDICOTT," 297 TONS, BUILT AT SALEM
IN 1819.
From a painting made in 1832. Altered to a bark in 1836.

[119] LETTER OF MARQUE BRIG "GRAND TURK," OF SALEM, 309 TONS,
BUILT AT WISCASSET, MAINE, IN 1812.
From a water-color by Anton Roux showing the vessel saluting at Marseilles in 1815.

The Letter of Marque Grand Turk of 18 Guns William Austin Commander, at Marseilles Harbour 1815.

The Letter of Marque Grand Turk of 14 Guns William Austin Commander at Marseilles Harbour 1815

[120] LETTER OF MARQUE BRIG "GRAND TURK," OF SALEM, 309 TONS, BUILT AT WISCASSET, MAINE, IN 1812.

From a water-color painted in 1815 by Anton Roux, showing the vessel at anchor at Marseilles.

[121] SHIP "GRAND TURK," OF SALEM, 300 TONS, BUILT ON
THE MASSACHUSETTS SOUTH SHORE, IN 1781.
Painting in an Oriental Lowestoft ware punch bowl made at Canton in 1786,
now at the Peabody Museum, Salem.

[122] SHIP "GRAVINA," OF BOSTON, 820 TONS, BUILT AT HOBOKEN, N. J., IN 1853, CAPT. CALEB SPRAGUE, MASTER.

[123] SHIP "GREAT ADMIRAL," 1575 TONS, BUILT AT EAST BOSTON IN 1869.

[124] SHIP "GREAT REPUBLIC, 3356 TONS, BUILT BY DONALD McKAY AT EAST BOSTON IN 1853.

Was 325 feet long and the largest of all the clippers. Partly destroyed by fire in New York, rebuilt and finally sold to English owners. Renamed the "Denmark" and abandoned at sea in 1872 on a voyage from Rio Janeiro.

[125] BARK "GYPSY," SAMUEL GRAVES
OF MARBLEHEAD, MASTER, ENTERING MARSEILLES,
DEC. 15, 1842.

[126] BARK "HAMILTON," OF SALEM, 275 TONS, BUILT AT
CAMDEN, MAINE, IN 1846.
From a water-color by Raffael Corsini, painted May 6, 1849 at Smyrna.

[127] BRIG "HAMILTON," OF SALEM, 164 TONS, BUILT AT
SCITUATE IN 1830.
From an oil painting by William Henry Luscomb of Salem, made about 1840.

[128] PRIVATEER BRIG "HARPY," 350 TONS, COMMANDED
BY CAPT. WILLIAM NICHOLS OF NEWBURYPORT.

[129] SCHOONER "HENRY R. TILTON," OF BELFAST, ME.,
492 TONS, BUILT AT WILMINGTON, DEL., IN 1875.

From a photograph showing the vessel ashore on Stony Beach,
Hull, in 1898.

[130] BARK "HAZARD," OF SALEM, 337 TONS, BUILT AT BOSTON
IN 1848.
Lost on Old Man's Shoal off Nantucket, Feb. 14, 1881. Famous for
her fast voyages.

[131] SHIP "HERCULES," OF SALEM, 290 TONS, BUILT AT HAVERHILL
IN 1805
From a water-color by "T. P." showing the ship "laying to in a heavy gale in
the Baltic, Nov. 6, 1825."

[132] SHIP "HERCULES," 290 TONS, BUILT AT HAVERHILL IN 1805.

[133] BRIG "HERSCHEL," JOHN DAVIS, MASTER.
Abandoned at sea in 1836.   From a water-color painted at Marseilles in 1825 by
Anton Roux.

[134] TOPSAIL-SCHOONER "H. H. COLE," OF SALEM, 98 TONS,
BUILT AT BALTIMORE IN 1843.
Lost in a collision at sea, Jan. 11, 1848. From an oil painting by Clement
Drew at the Peabody Museum, Salem.

[135] SHIP "HIGHLANDER," OF SALEM, 1352 TONS, BUILT AT
AT BOSTON IN 1869.
From an oil painting by a Chinese artist at Hong Kong, now at the
Peabody Museum, Salem.

[136] SHIP "HOPE," OF BOSTON, BUILT AT MEDFORD IN 1804
BY T. MAGOON.

[137] SHIP "HOPE," OF PROVIDENCE, R. I., OWNED
BY BROWN & IVES.

[138] SHIP "IDAHO," 998 TONS, BUILT AT EAST BOSTON IN 1860.

[139] BARK "IMAUM," 275 TONS, BUILT AT NEWBURYPORT IN 1850.

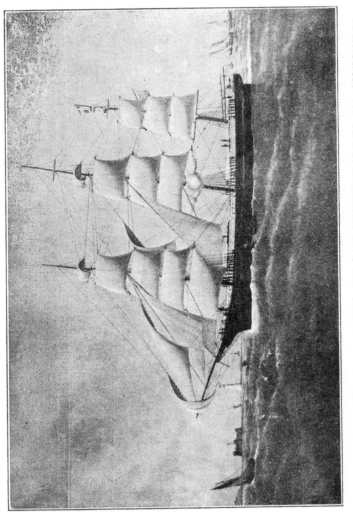

[140] SHIP "IMPORTER," 1276 TONS, BUILT AT NEWBURYPORT IN 1870, COMMANDED BY CAPT. GEORGE T. AVERY.

Engaged in the Calcutta trade. From a painting showing the ship passing Rock Light at the entrance to the river Mersey, Liverpool, England.

[141] BRIG "INCREASE," 108 TONS, COMMANDED IN 1803 BY CAPT. WILLIAM WIDGER OF MARBLEHEAD.

[142] CLIPPER-SHIP "INDEPENDENCE," 952 TONS, BUILT AT EAST BOSTON IN 1871.
From a photograph by Stebbins.

[143] SHIP "IRIS," OF SALEM, 227 TONS, BUILT AT KENNEBUNK,
MAINE, IN 1797.
From a water-color painted at Naples in 1806.

[144] BARK "ISABELLA," OWNED BY LOMBARD & CO., OF BOSTON.
Used in the Mediterranean trade and finally sunk by a privateer.

[145] SHIP "JAMES BAINES," 2515 TONS, BUILT AT EAST BOSTON BY DONALD McKAY, IN 1854, FOR JAMES BAINES & CO., OF LIVERPOOL.

A very fast clipper used in the Australian trade. In 1856 made 21 knots an hour. Burned at Liverpool and her hulk made into a landing stage.

[146] SHIP "JOHN," 258 TONS, BUILT AT SALEM, WITH A KETCH
RIG, IN 1795.
From a painting by M. F. Corne, 1803.

[147] BARK "JOHN WORSTER," 611 TONS, BUILT AT MEDFORD IN 1867.

[148] SHIP "JOHN BERTRAM," OF SALEM, 1080 TONS, BUILT AT EAST BOSTON IN 1851.
A fast sailing ship built in ninety days and used in the California trade. Went under the German flag in 1869.

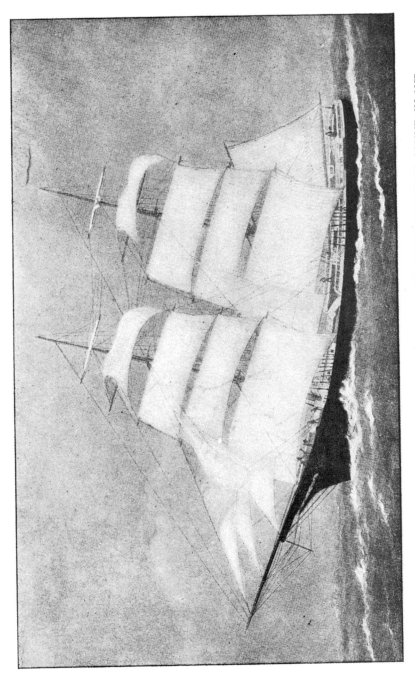

[149] BRIG "JOHN C. NOYES," OF NEWBURYPORT, 362 TONS, BUILT AT CALAIS, MAINE, IN 1875.

[150] HERMAPHRODITE BRIG "JOSEPH BALCH," OF BOSTON, 153 TONS, BUILT
AT MARSHFIELD IN 1840.

[151] SHIP "J. P. WHITNEY," 874 TONS, BUILT AT CASTINE, MAINE, IN 1852.
From a water-color made at Malta in 1864.

[152] LAUNCH OF THE BARKENTINE "JOSEPHINE," 939 TONS, BUILT AT BELFAST, MAINE, IN 1892. LOST ON HER MAIDEN TRIP.

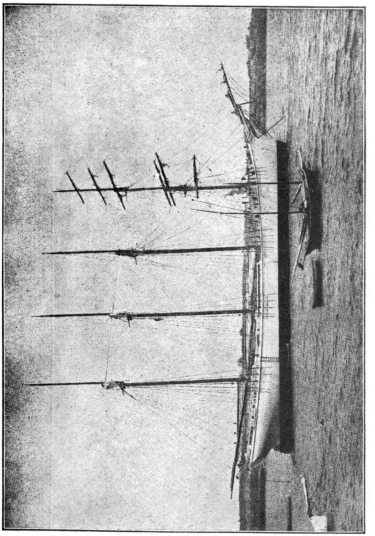

[153] FOUR-MASTED BARKENTINE "JOSEPHINE," 939 TONS, BUILT AT BELFAST, MAINE, IN 1892. A PINKY IS ANCHORED IN THE FOREGROUND.

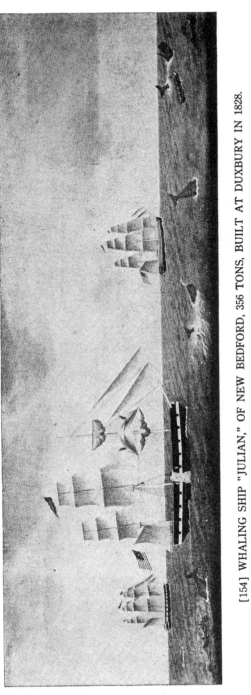

[154] WHALING SHIP "JULIAN," OF NEW BEDFORD, 356 TONS, BUILT AT DUXBURY IN 1828.

Half of a large oil painting at the Peabody Museum, Salem.

Juliana of Gloucester Capt. Abraham Williams

[155] BARK "JULIANA," OF GLOUCESTER, ABRAHAM WILLIAMS, MASTER.
From a water-color painted in 1807 by Nicolas Cammillieri.

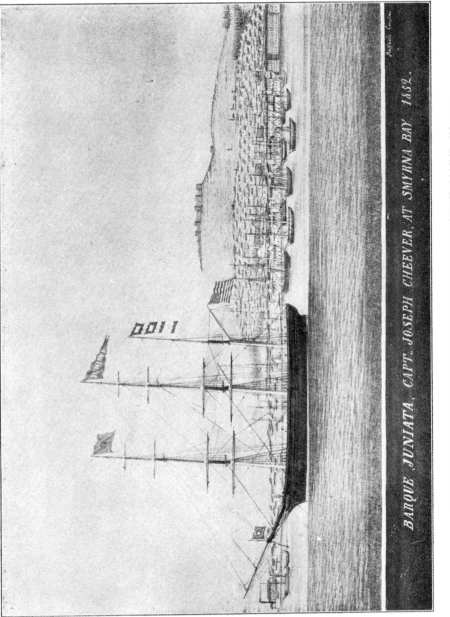

BARQUE JUNIATA, CAPT. JOSEPH CHEEVER, AT SMYRNA BAY 1852.

Raffaele Corsini

[156] BARK "JUANITA," 315 TONS, BUILT AT YARMOUTH, MAINE, IN 1844.
From a water-color painted at Smyrna in 1852 by Raffaele

[157] WHALING BARK "KATHLEEN," OF NEW BEDFORD, 205 TONS, BUILT AT
PHILADELPHIA IN 1844.

Attacked by a whale in 1902 and sunk in a few minutes.

[158] TOPSAIL-SCHOONER "KAMEHAMEHA III," 116 TONS,
BUILT AT BALTIMORE, MD., IN 1845 AND REGISTERED IN BOSTON.
Sold to the King of the Hawaiian Islands.

[159] WHALING SHIP "KUTUSOFF," 410 TONS, BUILT AT NEW BEDFORD
IN 1834.
A New Bedford whaler, condemned at Rio Janeiro in 1861.

[160] BARK "KEYSTONE," 568 TONS, BUILT AT PEMBROKE, MAINE, IN 1867.
From a painting showing the vessel off Holyhead.

[161] SHIP "LEADING WIND," 1208 TONS, BUILT AT BATH, MAINE, IN 1874.

[162] BRIG "LEANDER," 223 TONS, BUILT AT SALEM IN 1821.
From the water-color by Gi. Carmiletti at the Peabody Museum,
Salem, showing the ship entering Smyrna in 1830.

[163] BARK "LEO," COMMANDED BY CAPT. SAMUEL GRAVES
OF MARBLEHEAD.

[164] SHIP "LEODES," 445 TONS, BUILT AT KINGSTON IN 1841.
From a painting by J. Spise, Amsterdam, 1856, showing the vessel
entering Browershaven, May 19, 1856, from Samarang.

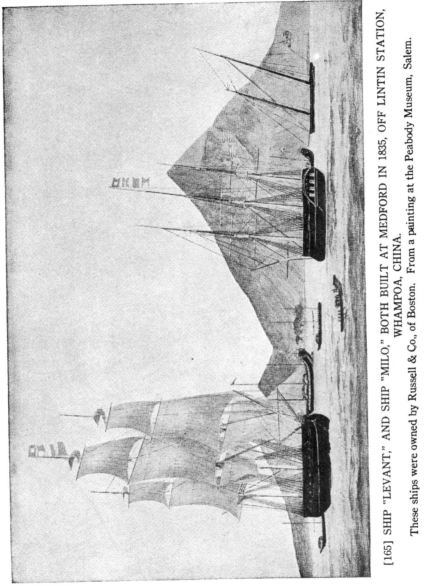

[165] SHIP "LEVANT," AND SHIP "MILO," BOTH BUILT AT MEDFORD IN 1835, OFF LINTIN STATION, WHAMPOA, CHINA.

These ships were owned by Russell & Co., of Boston. From a painting at the Peabody Museum, Salem.

[166] SCHOONER "LIDIA" 117 TONS, BUILT AT AMESBURY IN 1804.
From a water-color by Nicolas Cammillieri, showing the vessel
entering Marseilles, Nov. 10, 1807.

[167] SHIP "LIGHTNING," 2083 TONS, BUILT AT EAST BOSTON,
BY DONALD McKAY IN 1854.
Holds the world's record of 436 nautical miles for a day's run.
From a painting by Capt. W. B. Whall.

[168] SHIP "LIVERPOOL," 450 TONS, BUILT AT MEDFORD IN 1828.

[169] SHIP "LIVERPOOL," 450 TONS, BUILT AT MEDFORD
IN 1828.
From a painting by Robert Salmon, at the Peabody Museum, Salem.

[170] SHIP "LIVING AGE," OF BOSTON, 758 TONS, BUILT AT MEDFORD IN 1848. WRECKED ON PRATAS SHOAL IN THE CHINA SEA IN 1853.
From a painting by Marshall Johnson.

[171] SHIP "LOOCHOO," 639 TONS, BUILT AT MEDFORD IN 1840.

[172] HEMAPHRODITE-BRIG "LUBRA," OF BOSTON, 318 TONS,
BUILT AT DANVERSPORT IN 1864.

Lucilla of Boston – bound for China 1830.

Lucilla of Boston - bound for China 1830.

[173] SHIP "LUCILLA," OF BOSTON, 279 TONS, BUILT AT MEDFORD IN 1828.

From a water-color painted in 1830 by I. B. Melboro—.

[174] CLIPPER-SHIP "LUCY S. WILLIS," 1409 TONS, BUILT AT
EAST BOSTON IN 1869.
From an oil painting by Samuel Walters.

[175] BRIG "LYDIA," OF PLYMOUTH, MASSACHUSETTS.

[176] BRIG "MAGOUN," 180 TONS, BUILT AT MEDFORD IN 1825.
From a water-color by Frederic Roux painted at Marseilles in 1826.

[177] PINKY "MAINE," 24 TONS, BUILT AT ESSEX, MASS., IN 1845.
A type of small vessel once in general use along the New England
coast both for freighting and fishing.   From a
photograph taken in Belfast, Me., harbor.

[178] BRIG "MALAY," 268 TONS, BUILT AT SALEM IN 1818.
From a water-color by Peter Mazzinghi, showing
the brig at Leghorn, Oct. 16, 1831.

[179] SHIP "MALAY," 868 TONS, BUILT AT CHELSEA IN 1852.
From a painting showing the ship entering Hong Kong, Jan. 25, 1858.

[180] SHIP "MARGARET," 295 TONS, BUILT AT SALEM IN 1800.
From a water-color painted in 1802 by M. F. Corne.   Was in Japan
in July 1801.   Lost at sea in 1810.

[181] BRIG "MARIA," OF BOSTON, JOSEPH SAUNDERS, MASTER.
From a water-color by Anton Roux, painted in 1804 at Marseilles.

[182] SHIP "MARY," 1149 TONS, BUILT AT MARBLEHEAD IN 1854.
From a picture painted in 1879 by William York.

[183] BRIG "MARY HELEN" OF SALEM, 157 TONS, BUILT AT
HINGHAM IN 1833.

[184] SHIP "MARY L. CUSHING," 1575 TONS, BUILT AT NEWBURYPORT IN 1883.

[185] BRIG "MARY PAULINE," OF SALEM, 172 TONS, BUILT AT
HARTFORD, CONN., IN 1833.
Said to have been formerly a slaver under the name "Lalla Rookh."

[186] SHIP "MASSACHUSETTS," 344 TONS, BUILT AT SALISBURY IN 1805.
From an oil painting showing the ship entering the port of Leghorn, Jan. 8, 1807.

[187] THREE-MASTED TOPSAIL-SCHOONER "MAY,"
MULFORD PATTERSON, JR., MASTER.

[188] BRIG "MERCURY," COMMANDED BY CAPT. JOHN DEVEREUX
OF MARBLEHEAD, ENTERING ELSINEUR ROADS PROM BOSTON,
OCT. 11, 1825.

[189] BARK "METIS," 620 TONS, BUILT AT NEWBURYPORT IN 1868.
From an oil painting by W. H. Smith, at the Peabody Museum, Salem.

[190] BRIG "MEXICAN," 227 TONS, BUILT AT SALEM IN 1824.
SHOWING HER ATTACKED BY PIRATES, SEPT. 20, 1832,
WHILE ON A VOYAGE TO RIO JANEIRO.
From a painting made about 1876 by George Southward after a drawing
made in September, 1832 by Benjamin B. Reed.

[191] SHIP "MINDORO," OF SALEM, 1065 TONS, BUILT AT BOSTON IN 1854.
The last ship owned in Salem to engage in foreign trade. Sailed from Salem, April, 1897,
for the last time. A painting by Charles Torrey, at the Peabody Museum, Salem.

[192] SHIP "MINDORO," 1065 TONS, BUILT IN 1864
AT BOSTON.

[193] SHIP "MOREA," 330 TONS, BUILT AT CHARLESTOWN IN 1828.
From a painting by Walter and Son, 7 Pleasant St., Liverpool,
dated July 13, 1830.

[194] SHIP "MONK," OF SALEM, 253 TONS, BUILT AT
NOBLEBOROUGH, MAINE, IN 1805.
From a water-color after the original painting by Nicolai Carmillieri,
Marseilles, 1806.

[195] TOPSAIL-SCHOONER "MISSIONARY PACKET," 40
TONS, BUILT AT SALEM IN 1825.

[196] SHIP "MOUNT HOPE," OF NEWPORT, R. I.
From a drawing made in 1801 in a log book now in the possession of the
Massachusetts Historical Society.

[197] SHIP "MOUNT VERNON," 355 TONS, BUILT AT SALEM IN 1798.
From a water-color painted in 1799 by M. F. Corne.

[198] SHIP "MOUNT VERNON," 355 TONS, BUILT AT SALEM IN 1798.
From a water-color painted in 1799 by M. F. Corne, showing an encounter
with a French cruiser.

[199] SHIP "MOUNT VERNON," 355 TONS, BUILT AT SALEM IN 1798.
From a water-color by M. F. Corne, 1799, showing an engagement
with a French latteener.

[200] BRIG "NAIAD," OF SALEM, 259 TONS, BUILT AT HAVERHILL
IN 1817.
From a water-color by Anton Roux painted in 1820.

[201] BRIG "NANCY," OF MARBLEHEAD, 150 TONS.
From a water-color by Anton Roux painted at Marseilles in 1823.

202] SHIP "NANCY," BUILT AT NEWBURY IN 1802.
From a water-color by F. Dannenberg, 1805.

[203] BARK "NATCHEZ," 299 TONS, BUILT IN 1838.
From a painting at the Peabody Museum, Salem.

Brig Nancy Ann Rich: Cleveland Commander

[204] BRIG "NANCY ANN," OF SALEM, 173 TONS, BUILT AT SALISBURY IN 1809,
RICHARD CLEVELAND, MASTER.

[205] SHIP "NAVIGATOR," 333 TONS, BUILT AT MEDFORD IN 1841.
From a painting destroyed in the great Salem fire of 1915.

[206] BRIG "NEREUS," OF SALEM, 181 TONS, BUILT AT
HAVERHILL IN 1818.

[207] SHIP "NIGHTINGALE," 1066 TONS, BUILT AT
PORTSMOUTH, N. H., IN 1851.
Built as an exhibit for the International Exposition at London.
Used in the China trade and in 1861 became a slaver.

[208] SHIP "NIOBE," 686 TONS, BUILT AT MEDFORD IN 1847.

[209] SHIP "NORTH BEND," 365 TONS, BUILT AT HAVERHILL IN 1841.
From a painting by J. Spinn of Amsterdam, showing the brig "entering the Texel, 1842."

[210] SHIP "NORTHERN CHIEF," 1136 TONS, BUILT AT BELFAST,
MAINE, IN 1852.
Used in the California trade.

[211] SHIP "OCEANA," 631 TONS, BUILT AT MEDFORD IN 1840.
From a water-color by Frederick Roux made at Havre in April, 1841.

[212] SHIP "OCEAN QUEEN," 824 TONS, BUILT AT NEWBURYPORT IN 1847.

[213] SHIP "OCEAN ROVER," 776 TONS, BUILT AT
PORTSMOUTH, N. H., IN 1860.
From a painting showing the ship entering Hong Kong, Feb. 20, 1865.

[214] BRIG "OLINDA," 178 TONS, BUILT AT SALEM IN 1825.
From a water-color by Francois Roux, now at the Peabody Museum, Salem.

Brig "Olive" of Newburyport. Murysk [illegible] forc'masts entering Leghorn Roads 15 "1819.

[215] BRIG "OLIVE," 157 TONS, BUILT AT NEWBURY IN 1815.
From a water-color showing the brig entering Leghorn Roads, Feb. 18, 1819.

[216] BRIG "ORIENTAL," 195 TONS, BUILT AT BOSTON IN 1832.
Owned by Capt. Charles Hoffman of Salem.   From a painting by Robert Salmon.

[217] SHIP "OROONDATES," 1768 TONS, BUILT AT SWANZEY, MASS.
IN 1855, AND OWNED BY C. & J. MARUAN OF PROVIDENCE.
From a painting showing the ship at Antwerp.

[218] SHIP "PALESTINE," AUGUSTUS V. LITTLEFIELD, MASTER.
From a water-color by Frederic Roux showing the ship leaving Havre, Aug. 1, 1840.

[219] BARK "PATRIOT," 255 TONS, BUILT AT DANVERS IN 1809.
From a painting made in 1817 by Jacob Petersen.

[220] SHIP "PEPPERELL," 668 TONS, BUILT AT BIDDEFORD,
MAINE IN 1854.

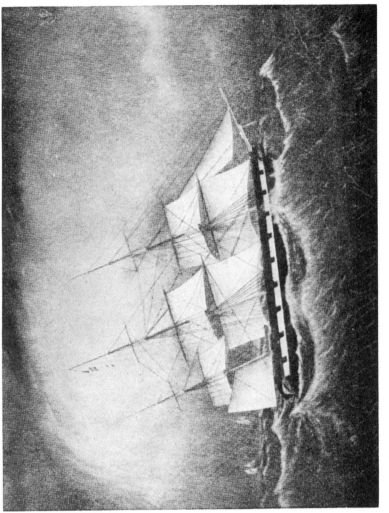

[221] SHIP "PAUL JONES," 624 TONS, BUILT AT MEDFORD IN 1842, COMMANDED BY CAPT. DANIEL C. BACON.

[222] BRIGANTINE "PEGGY," OF SALEM, 167 TONS,
BUILT AT BERWICK, MAINE,
IN 1788.
From the picture on a pitcher of Liverpool ware made in
1797. Probably a typical rather than an actual portrait.

[223] BRIG "PERSEVERANCE," 184 TONS, BUILT AT PEMBROKE, MAINE, IN 1815.
From a water-color painted in 1836 by Frederic Roux, at Marseilles.

[224] SHIP "PERSEVERANCE," 245 TONS, BUILT AT
HAVERHILL IN 1794.
Wrecked on Cape Cod in 1805.

[225] BRIG "PERSIA," 254 TONS, BUILT AT SALEM IN 1822.
Wrecked on Cape Ann in 1829 and all hands perished.

[226] BRIG "PHOENIX," 248 TONS, BUILT AT NEWBURY IN 1816.
From a water-color by Antoine Vittaluga, painted at Genoa in January, 1829.

[227] UNITED STATES JACKASS-BRIG "PICKERING," OF NEWBURYPORT,
187 TONS, BUILT AT BOSTON IN 1798. LOST AT SEA IN 1800.

[228] BRIG "PICO," 210 TONS, BUILT AT PEMBROKE, MAINE, IN 1851.
From a painting by Robert W. Salmon, made about 1840, showing the brig lying in
the harbor of Fayal, with Pico mountain in the distance.

[229] BARK "PROMPT," OF BOSTON, 197 TONS, BUILT AT WEYMOUTH IN 1841.

[230] SCHOONER "POLLY," BUILT IN 1805.
From a photograph made in 1904 in Belfast, Maine, harbor.

[231] SCHOONER "POLLY," 48 TONS, BUILT AT AMESBURY IN 1805.
The oldest schooner still afloat.   From a photograph made in New York harbor.

[232] SHIP "PROPONTIS," OF SALEM, 425 TONS, BUILT AT
MEDFORD IN 1833.

[233] BRIG "PRUDENT," OF BOSTON ON MARCH 26, 1820,
COMMANDED BY CAPT. BENJAMIN GRAVES OF MARBLEHEAD.

[234] SHIP "PRUDENT," 214 TONS, BUILT AT SALEM IN 1899.
From an old water-color at the Peabody Museum, Salem.

[235] SHIP "RADUGA," 586 TONS, BUILT AT NEWBURY IN 1848.
From a drawing made in 1863.

[236] SHIP "RADIANT," 1318 TONS, BUILT AT EAST BOSTON IN 1852, FOR BAKER AND MORRILL OF BOSTON.

This ship was wrecked on Crocodile Reef in 1871, while on a voyage from Singapore to Boston.

[237] SHIP "RADIANT," 1318 TONS; AND SHIP "JOHN LAND,"
1064 TONS, BUILT AT SOUTH BOSTON IN 1853.

THE SCHOONER RAVEN. MARBLEHEAD. AMBROS B MARTIN MASTER

[238] SCHOONER "RAVEN," 70 TONS, COMMANDED IN 1896
BY CAPT. AMBROSE B. MARTIN OF MARBLEHEAD.

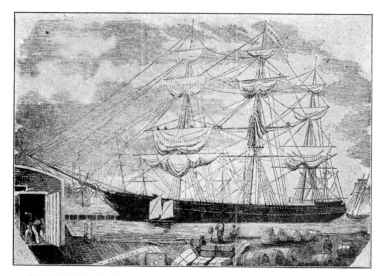

[239] SHIP "R. B. FORBES," OF BOSTON, 748 TONS, BUILT
AT BOSTON IN 1851.
Sold in 1863 at Hong Kong to foreign owners.

[240] BRIG "REAPER," OF SALEM, 229 TONS, BUILT AT
AMESBURY IN 1820.
From a water-color by Anton Roux, Jr., painted at Marseilles in 1823.

[241] SHIP "RECOVERY," 284 TONS, BUILT AT SALEM IN 1794.
From a painting made in 1799 by William Ward.   The first
American vessel to visit Mocha.

[242] SHIP "RED JACKET," 2030 TONS, BUILT AT
ROCKLAND, MAINE, IN 1853.
A famous Australian packet of the White Star Line.

[243] BARK "RICHARD," 252 TONS, BUILT AT SALEM IN 1826.
From a water-color painted in 1831 at Marseilles by H. Pellegrin,
now at the Peabody Museum, Salem.

[244] SHIP "ROBERT H. DIXEY," 1253 TONS, BUILT AT
EAST BOSTON IN 1855.
Lost Sept. 15, 1860 on Mobile bar.

[245] SHIP "REPORTER," 1474 TONS, BUILT AT EAST BOSTON IN 1853.
A very fast clipper used in the California trade.   Abandoned off Cape Horn in 1862.

[246] BARK "RICHARD," 252 TONS, BUILT AT SALEM IN 1826, WHALING IN THE SOUTH PACIFIC IN 1837.

Part of a painting at the Peabody Museum, Salem.

[247] SHIP "ROME," 344 TONS, BUILT AT SALEM IN 1829.
From a water-color by H. Pellegrin showing the ship leaving Marseilles
in March, 1848.

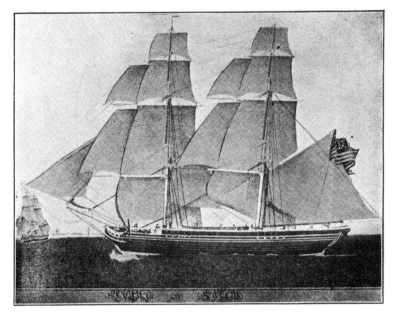

[248] BRIG "ROQUE," OF SALEM, 206 TONS, BUILT AT
JONESBOROUGH, MAINE, IN 1816.
From a water-color probably painted at Palermo.

[249] SHIP "ROSANNA," 283 TONS, BUILT AT DUXBURY IN 1827.
From a painting made in 1828.

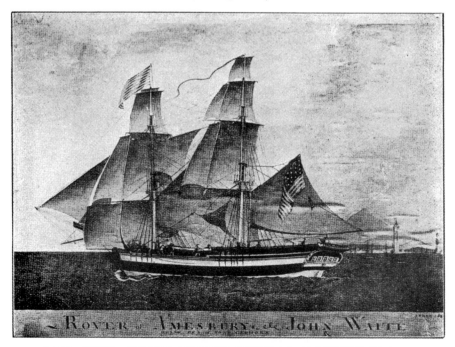

[250] SNOW "ROVER," 161 TONS, BUILT AT AMESBURY IN 1803.

[251] SHIP "ST. PATRICK," 1149 TONS, BUILT AT WARREN, MAINE, IN 1852.
Wrecked on the New Jersey coast about 1860.

[252] SHIP "ST. PAUL," 463 TONS, BUILT AT BOSTON IN 1833.
Lost in the Philippine Islands, Dec. 9, 1851.

[253] SHIP "SALLY," OF SALEM, 322 TONS, BUILT AT BOSTON IN 1803.
From a water-color probably made in 1803 at Palermo or Genoa.

[254] SHIP "SAMUEL RUSSEL," 957 TONS, BUILT IN 1846.
One of the fastest clippers of her day.   Lost off the Cape of Good Hope.
From a painting in the Nantucket Library.

[255] SHIP "SALLY ANNE," OF BOSTON, 312 TONS, BUILT AT BRAINTREE IN 1804.
Became a New Bedford whaler in 1846 and was wrecked on the Friendly Islands, Apr. 2, 1854.

[256] SHIP "SAPPHIRE," OF SALEM, 365 TONS, BUILT AT MEDFORD
IN 1824.
A whaler from Salem in 1836 - 1842 ; foundered in the West Indies, Mar. 8, 1842,
while on a voyage to Mobile.

[257] BARK "SAPPHO," OF SALEM, 319 TONS, BUILT AT BOSTON
IN 1844.

[258] BARK "SARAH," OF BOSTON, OWNED BY E. A. ADAMS
AND USED IN THE AZORES TRADE.

[259] BRIGANTINE "SEAMAN," OF GLOUCESTER, LEAVING
MARSEILLES FOR THE GULF OF MEXICO, MAY, 1825.
From a water-color by Anton Roux, Jr.

[260] SHIP "SHIRLEY," OF SALEM, 910 TONS, BUILT AT
MEDFORD IN 1850.
From an oil painting by a Chinese artist at Hong Kong.

[261] SHIP "SIAM," 727 TONS, BUILT AT PORTSMOUTH, N. H.
IN 1847.
From a painting by a Chinese artist.

[262] SHIP "SOOLOO," 440 TONS, BUILT AT SALEM IN 1840.
From a water-color by H. Pellegrini showing the ship entering the harbor
of Marseilles ln 1844.

[263] SHIP "SOOLOO" (2d), OF SALEM, 784 TONS, BUILT AT
BOSTON IN 1861.
From a photograph showing the ship leaving Boston for San Francisco
on June 1, 1861.

[264] SHIP "SOUTHERN CROSS," 1000 TONS, BUILT AT SOUTH BOSTON IN 1851.

[265] SHIP "SOVEREIGN OF THE SEAS," 2421 TONS, BUILT
AT EAST BOSTON IN 1852.

[266] SHIP "SPARTAN," 475 TONS, BUILT AT NEWBURY IN 1834.
From a water-color by Frederic Roux, showing the ship leaving Havre, May 26, 1836.

[267] SHIP "STAG HOUND," OF BOSTON, 1535 TONS, BUILT
AT EAST BOSTON IN 1850.
Built for the California trade.   Burned at sea in 1863 off the coast
of Brazil.

[268] SHIP "STAFFORDSHIRE," OF BOSTON, 1817 TONS, BUILT AT EAST BOSTON IN 1851, FOR ENOCH TRAIN & CO.

Used in the Liverpool and California trades. Wrecked on Blonde Rock, near Cape Sable, with the loss of 170 lives.

[269] BARK "STAR," OF SALEM, 212 TONS, BUILT AT SCITUATE
IN 1838.
From an oil painting at the Peabody Museum, Salem, probably by
Benjamin F. West of Salem.

[270] SHIP "STARLIGHT," 1150 TONS, BUILT AT SOUTH
BOSTON IN 1854.
Sold to Italian owners and renamed "Proto Longo."

[271] SHIP "STREGLITZ," COMMANDED BY CAPT.
DANIEL T. LOTHROP OF COHASSET.

[272] BRIGANTINE "SUKEY," OF SALEM, 102 TONS, BUILT AT
FALMOUTH, MASS. IN 1795.
Probably sold in Russia in 1812.   From a painting made in 1802 by
George Ropes of Salem.

[273] SHIP "SUMATRA," OF SALEM, 1041 TONS, BUILT AT
CHELSEA IN 1856.
From an oil painting by an English artist showing the ship off the cliffs
of Dover, on Sept. 12, 1857.

[274] SHIP "SUNNY SOUTH," 703 TONS,
COMMANDED IN 1853 BY CAPT. MICHAEL B.
GREGORY OF MARBLEHEAD.
From a painting by Thomas Pitman.

[275] SHIP "SYREN," OF SALEM, 1064 TONS, BUILT AT MEDFORD IN 1851.
From a photograph taken at New Bedford.

[276] SHIP "SYREN," OF SALEM, 1064 TONS, BUILT AT MEDFORD IN 1851.
From a painting by a Chinese artist made at Hong Kong in 1855, showing the ship near Lintin Island.

[277] BRIG "TALISMAN," 240 TONS, BUILT AT MEDFORD IN 1822.

[278] RESCUE IN 1856 IN MID-OCEAN OF THE CREW OF THE
SHIP "TEJUCA," BY THE SHIP "EXCELSIOR," 444 TONS, BUILT
AT KENNEBUNK, MAINE, IN 1845.
From a painting by Thomas Pitman.

[279] SHIP "TELEMACHUS," OF BOSTON, CAPT. JOHN CLARK
OF SALEM, MASTER.
Frnm a water-color by Anton Roux, painted at Marseilles in 1805.

[280] BRIG "TELEMACHUS," OF SALEM AND BOSTON, 133 TONS,
BUILT AT NEW YORK IN 1798.

[281] TOPSAIL SCHOONER "THETIS," OF BOSTON, OFF THE
COAST OF SICILY.
From a water-color painted in 1822 by Zi. Eruzione.

[282] SHIP "THOMAS PERKINS," OF SALEM, 595 TONS, BUILT AT
PORTSMOUTH, N. H., IN 1837.

[283] HERMAPHRODITE BRIG "THOOSA," 110 TONS, COMMANDED
BY CAPT. MICHAEL B. POWERS OF MARBLEHEAD.
From a water-color made at Smyrna in 1835.

[284] BARK "TIDAL WAVE," 361 TONS, BUILT AT ESSEX IN 1854.
From a photograph taken about 1862 showing the vessel laying at
Webb's Wharf, Salem.

[285] SHIP "TOM," COMMANDED BY CAPT. JOHN
BAILEY OF MARBLEHEAD.
Painted about 1800 on a Staffordshire plate.

[286] SHIP "TITAN," 1985 TONS, BUILT AT NEW YORK IN 1855, OWNED BY
D. G. & W. BACON OF BOSTON.

Used in the Australian trade and abandoned at sea Feb. 16, 1858. The picture shows her coming into
Liverpool after having lost her main and mizzen masts in a gale.

[287] SNOW "TOPAZ," 213 TONS, BUILT AT NEWBURY IN 1807.
From a water-color painted by Anton Roux at Marseilles in 1808.

[288] SHIP "TRENT," OF SALEM, 191 TONS, BUILT AT
FREEPORT, MAINE, IN 1801.

[289] SHIP "TRIUMPHANT," OF SALEM, 203 TONS, BUILT AT
DOVER, N. H. IN 1802.
From a large oil painting by George Ropes, 1805, at the Peabody Museum, Salem.

[290] SHIP "TWO BROTHERS," 288 TONS, BUILT AT
SALEM IN 1818.
From a water-color by George Ropes of Salem, painted in 1818, now at
the Peabody Museum, Salem.

[291] SHIP "TYPHOON," 1610 TONS, BUILT AT
PORTSMOUTH, N. H.
Launched fully rigged with colors flying.

[292] SHIP "ULYSSES" (1st), OF SALEM, 163 TONS, BUILT AT
AMESBURY IN 1794.
Wrecked on Cape Cod, Feb. 22, 1802. From a water-color by M. F. Corne.

[293] SHIP "ULYSSES" (2d), OF SALEM, 340 TONS, BUILT AT
HAVERHILL IN 1798.
From a water-color by Anton Roux, painted at Marseilles in 1804, showing the
temporary rudder by means of which the ship safely reached that port.

[294] SHIP "ULYSSES" (2d), OF SALEM, 340 TONS.
From a water-color by Anton Roux, showing the ship entering the
harbor of Marseilles, Mar. 23, 1804.

[295] BRIG "UNCAS," OF BOSTON, 227 TONS.
From a painting on glass done at Antwerp by P. Weyts.

[296] SLOOP "UNION," OF BOSTON.
From a drawing made in 1795 in a log-book now at the Massachusetts
Historical Society.

[297] SHIP "UNION," 250 TONS, BUILT AT SALEM IN 1802.
Lost on Baker's Island, Salem harbor, Feb. 24, 1817.

[298] SHIP "VOLUSIA," OF SALEM, 273 TONS, BUILT AT
FALMOUTH, MASS. IN 1801.
Wrecked on Cape Cod, Feb. 22, 1802.   From a water-color by M. F. Corne.

[299] BARK "WASHINGTON," OF MARBLEHEAD, 135 TONS,
COMMANDED BY CAPT. JOHN BAILEY IN 1796.
From an India ink drawing made at Nice.

[300] BRIG "WATER WITCH," 167 TONS, BUILT AT SCITUATE
IN 1831.
From a water-color showing the brig at Smyrna, Sept. 15, 1832.

[301] SHIP "WESTWARD HO," 1650 TONS, BUILT AT
EAST BOSTON IN 1851.
Burned at Callao, Feb. 27, 1864.

[302] BRIG "WHIG," OF BOSTON, FRANCIS H. ROGERS, MASTER.
From a water-color painted at Palermo.

[303] BARK "WILLIAM SCHRODER," 238 TONS, BUILT AT
COHASSET IN 1840.
From an oil painting by Benjamin F. West of Salem.

[304] BARK "WITCH," 210 TONS, BUILT AT SALEM IN 1854.
From a painting by a Chinese artist framed in typical Chinese manner.

[305] SHIP "WITCHCRAFT," OF SALEM AND BOSTON, 1311 TONS, BUILT
AT CHELSEA, IN 1852.
Wrecked off Cape Hatteras in 1861.

[306] SHIP "WITCHCRAFT," OF SALEM AND BOSTON,
1311 TONS, BUILT AT CHELSEA IN 1852.
Wrecked off Cape Hatteras in 1861.

[307] SHIP "WITCH OF THE WAVE," OF 1498 TONS, BUILT
AT PORTSMOUTH, N. H., IN 1851.
Used in the California and China trades.   Sold at Amsterdam in 1856.

[308] BARK "ZOTOFF," OF SALEM, 220 TONS, BUILT AT NEWBURY,
MASS., IN 1840.
Used in the Feejee, South American and Cayenne trades.